M000094583

curry
recipe collection
by Sainsbury's

A collection of 100 simple curries,
starters, side dishes and desserts

Welcome...

to the curry recipe collection by Sainsbury's.

Everyone loves a curry. But why get a takeaway when it's just as easy to make your own at home! This collection of delicious recipes brings together some of the most popular curry dishes from around the world – plus a few lesser known ones to try. We're also delighted to have teamed up with *Sainsbury's magazine* to bring you six of their best curry recipes as well.

As always, we've tried, tested and tasted each recipe so you can be sure of great results every time. To make things easier, we've arranged the book in clear sections from starters, mains (by main ingredient), sides through to desserts, with the recipes arranged within each chapter from quick to slow so you'll know how long each will take you to make. To get ahead, we've included recipes for the most popular curry paste bases, along with a comprehensive ingredients glossary to expand your knowledge of the spices, herbs and storecupboard favourites used in these wonderful dishes.

Happy cooking!

contents

We've added icons to make everything as clear as possible:

 Our one to three chilli heat rating system will tell you how hot each curry is

 Suitable for vegetarians

 Recipes containing 1 or more of your 5-a-day, to help you plan for healthier eating. Try to eat at least 5 different portions of fruit and veg a day. Fresh, frozen, dried, canned and juice all count.

For an explanation of the nutritional breakdown of each recipe featured, please turn to p193. Nutrition is calculated using each recipe's ingredients list only and does not include any sides, accompaniments or other serving suggestions mentioned in the method.

Freezer information: All the main dish curries can be frozen. Put into freezable container when cool and freeze for up to 1 month. Defrost thoroughly overnight in the fridge and cook until piping hot throughout.

Sainsbury's encourages responsible drinking – visit DRINKAWARE.CO.UK

Discover a world of flavour

Before you cook, find out about the origins of curry and what makes it so unique and well-loved...

To most of us, curry is synonymous with India. So it can come as a bit of a surprise to learn that the word 'curry' isn't even used in India. So where did it come from and why are we using it? There are some who believe it evolved from the Tamil word 'kari', meaning stew, or that it originated from the Hindi name for their circular steel cooking vessels, or 'karahi'. Either way, it's fair to say that it was the British – more specifically, traders from the East India Company – who first used the term to describe the food they encountered while setting up their commercial outposts along India's provincial coastlines in the 17th century.

While the origin of the word may be something of a minor mystery, 'curry' has evolved to become a generic British term to cover all manner of spicy foods – either cooked in a 'wet' sauce or dry spiced foods. And wherever the British have traded since arriving in India in the 1600s, they have taken the 'curry' concept with them. So these days you're as likely to find a curry dish in a Jamaican, African or Malaysian restaurant as you are in an Indian one. No cuisine has travelled so well and so far!

Take the spice route

Our celebration of curry includes all your Indian takeaway menu favourites, plus the best from South-East Asia, Indonesia, the Caribbean and beyond. The one element common to them all is spice. The subtle combination, quantities

and variety of spices used is what makes each curry unique, with the differences from country to country coming from the availability of ingredients and local tastes, as well as religious considerations. So a Japanese katsu curry draws its influence from distinctly oriental ingredients, such as soy sauce and mirin, while Caribbean curries use sweet potatoes, coconut milk and native chillies, such as Scotch Bonnets, to give them their special flavour. Recipes from the Indian subcontinent make use of a variety of spices, including cumin, coriander, turmeric, mustard seeds, cinnamon and cardamom. And if you take a recipe from South-East Asia, you'll find the influence of lime leaves, lemon grass, galangal and fish sauce taking centre stage. Turn to our ingredients glossary on p184 to find out more about the incredible array of ingredients – both commonplace and unusual. All of the ingredients used in these recipes are available to buy at Sainsbury's and it's well worth seeking out the more unexpected ones to make these exceptional dishes.

Recipes you can trust

In the course of creating this book, we've researched, cooked and tasted our way through each and every recipe. Of course, all cooks have their own way of creating certain dishes, but we've done our best to re-create our versions in the most authentic way possible. Many of these recipes start with a paste base, and over the page you'll find the basic paste recipes you'll need for many of our curry recipes. These will keep for several days (if not longer), so you can get ahead if you like. And if you want to make cooking even faster, you'll find that Sainsbury's already makes many of these pastes for you to buy instore.

It's often thought that curries are time-consuming to make, with authentic results being tricky to achieve. However, the recipes here range from the very simple and quick to those that take a bit more time – but all are well within the capabilities of any keen home-cook. You'll be surprised how little kitchen equipment and techniques you'll need to create rewarding dishes that your family and friends will love. Read on and enjoy!

Pastes

A homemade curry paste will make all the difference to the finished dish. Prepare yours ahead and the flavours will intensify in the fridge

Jalfrezi paste Ⓥ

MAKES 110g (about 6 tbsp)
PREP TIME: 5 mins
COOK TIME: 1-2 mins

---

1 tsp mustard seeds
1 tsp ground turmeric
1 tsp ground fenugreek
1 green chilli, deseeded (optional) and
roughly chopped
2 tbsp tomato purée
3 tbsp chopped fresh coriander
2 cloves garlic, crushed
2cm piece fresh ginger,
peeled and chopped

---

1 Tip the mustard seeds into a heavy-based frying pan and toast over a medium heat for 1-2 mins, until just starting to pop.

2 Transfer the toasted seeds to a mini food processor with the remaining ingredients and 3 tbsp water. Blend to a paste. Store in a clean sealed jar (see cook's tips) in the fridge for up to 1 week.

The nutritional analysis for these pastes are included in the recipe breakdowns where they are used.

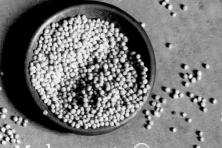

Madras paste Ⓥ

MAKES 125g (about 5 tbsp)
PREP TIME: 15 mins, plus cooling
COOK TIME: 2-3 mins

---

2 tbsp ground coriander
1 tsp ground black pepper
2 tsp hot chilli powder
1 tsp garam masala
1 tsp ground turmeric
1 tbsp ground cumin
2 cloves garlic, crushed
2 tbsp brown malt vinegar
1 tbsp vegetable oil

---

1   Mix the spices, garlic and vinegar in a small bowl with 5 tbsp water.

2   Heat the oil in a frying pan and add the spice paste. Fry over a medium heat for 2-3 mins, stirring, until reduced. Cool, then store in a clean sealed jar (see cook's tips) in the fridge for up to 2 weeks.

Goan masala paste Ⓥ

MAKES 65g (about 3 tbsp)
PREP TIME: 10 mins
COOK TIME: 1-2 mins

---

2 tsp cumin seeds
1 heaped tbsp coriander seeds
5 whole cloves
2 tsp black peppercorns
1 red chilli, deseeded and chopped
5 cloves garlic, crushed
2 tsp ground turmeric
2 tsp dark brown sugar
1 tbsp red wine vinegar

---

1   Put the cumin, coriander, cloves and peppercorns in a heavy-based frying pan. Toast over a medium heat for 1-2 mins, stirring, until lightly browned and aromatic.

2   Transfer the toasted spices to a mini food processor with the remaining ingredients and 4 tbsp water. Blend to a paste. Store in a clean sealed jar (see cook's tips) in the fridge for up to 2 weeks.

Balti paste Ⓥ

MAKES 125g (about 6 tbsp)
PREP TIME: 5 mins
COOK TIME: 1-2 mins

---

1 tsp cumin seeds
1 tsp mustard seeds
1 tbsp ground cinnamon
1 tbsp ground coriander
2 tsp ground turmeric
1 tsp smoked paprika
1 tsp ground fenugreek
½ tsp hot chilli powder
2 tbsp tomato purée

---

1   Put the cumin and mustard seeds in a heavy-based frying pan and toast over a medium heat for 1-2 mins, stirring, until lightly browned and aromatic.

2   Transfer the seeds to a mini food processor with the remaining ingredients and 100ml water. Blend to a paste. If the paste is too thick, add more water. Store in a clean sealed jar (see cook's tips) in the fridge for up to 2 weeks.

Korma paste Ⓥ

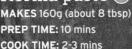

MAKES 160g (about 8 tbsp)
PREP TIME: 10 mins
COOK TIME: 2-3 mins

30g desiccated coconut
4 cardamom pods, crushed to release the seeds (discard the pods)
2 tsp fennel seeds
2 tsp ground cumin
1 tsp ground turmeric
1 red chilli, deseeded and chopped
15g macadamia nuts by Sainsbury's
2 shallots, peeled and chopped
1 tbsp vegetable oil
4-5cm piece fresh ginger, peeled and chopped

---

1   Heat a heavy-based frying pan over a medium heat. Add the desiccated coconut and toast for 1-2 mins, stirring, until lightly browned. Transfer to a mini food processor.

2   Add the cardamom and fennel seeds to the frying pan and toast over a medium heat for 1-2 mins, stirring, until lightly browned and aromatic. Transfer to the food processor with the remaining ingredients and 5 tbsp water. Blend to a paste. Store in a clean sealed jar (see cook's tips) in the fridge for up to 2 weeks.

Tandoori paste Ⓥ

MAKES 116g (about 6 tbsp)
PREP TIME: 5-10 mins

---

2 cloves garlic, crushed
2cm piece fresh ginger, peeled and finely grated
2 red chillies, deseeded and chopped
2 tbsp paprika
½ tsp garam masala
½ tsp ground turmeric
Juice of ½ lemon
1 tbsp groundnut oil

---

1   Put all the ingredients in a mini food processor with 3 tbsp water. Blend to a paste. Store in a clean sealed jar (see cook's tips) in the fridge for up to 2 weeks.

Tikka paste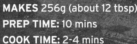

MAKES 125g (about 6 tbsp)
PREP TIME: 10 mins

3 cloves garlic, crushed
2cm piece fresh ginger, peeled and chopped
1 tsp smoked paprika
2 tbsp tomato purée
2 tsp garam masala
1 tsp ground turmeric
1 tsp ground coriander
1 tbsp desiccated coconut
2 red chillies, deseeded and finely chopped
1 tbsp groundnut oil

1 Put all the ingredients in a mini food processor with 3 tbsp water and blend to a paste. Store in a clean sealed jar (see cook's tips) in the fridge for up to 2 weeks.

Thai green curry paste

MAKES: 145g (about 7 tbsp)
PREP: 10 mins

2 stalks lemon grass, finely chopped
2 shallots, peeled and finely chopped
3 hot green bird eye chillies by Sainsbury's
30g fresh galangal by Sainsbury's, peeled and chopped
4 cloves garlic, crushed
3 fresh kaffir lime leaves by Sainsbury's, washed and roughly shredded
Handful fresh coriander, roughly chopped
½ tsp shrimp paste
1 tbsp vegetable oil

1 Add all the ingredients to a mini food processor with 4 tbsp water, season and blend to a paste. Store in a clean sealed jar (see cook's tips) in the fridge for up to 1 week.

Thai red curry paste

MAKES 135g (about 6 tbsp)

Follow the recipe for Thai green curry paste, replacing the green chilli with red chilli. Omit the coriander and add 1 tbsp paprika.

Thai yellow curry paste

MAKES 148g (about 7 tbsp)

Follow the recipe for Thai green curry paste, adding 2 tsp ground turmeric.

Rendang paste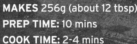

MAKES 256g (about 12 tbsp)
PREP TIME: 10 mins
COOK TIME: 2-4 mins

30g desiccated coconut
1 tbsp coriander seeds
1 tbsp cumin seeds
1 tsp ground turmeric
½ onion, finely chopped
4 cloves garlic, crushed
1 large red chilli, deseeded and finely chopped
30g fresh galangal by Sainsbury's, peeled and chopped
1 tbsp vegetable oil

1 Heat a heavy-based frying pan over a medium heat. Add the coconut and toast for 1-2 mins, until lightly browned. Transfer to a mini food processor.

2 Add the coriander and cumin seeds to the pan and toast over a medium heat for 1-2 mins, stirring, until lightly browned and aromatic. Transfer to the food processor with the remaining ingredients and 6 tbsp water. Blend to a paste. Store in a clean sealed jar (see cook's tips) in the fridge for up to 2 weeks.

Rogan josh paste

MAKES 100g (about 5 tbsp)
PREP TIME: 10 mins, plus cooling
COOK TIME: 2 mins

8 cardamom pods, crushed to release the seeds (discard the pods)
8 whole cloves
2 tsp ground cinnamon
1 tbsp ground cumin
1 tbsp ground coriander
1 tbsp fennel seeds, roughly crushed
1½ tsp hot chilli powder
1 tbsp vegetable oil

1 Put all the ingredients, except the oil, in a mini food processor with 6 tbsp water. Blend to a paste.

2 Heat the oil in a frying pan and add the spice paste. Fry over a medium heat for 2 mins, stirring. Cool, then store in a clean sealed jar (see cook's tips) in the fridge for up to 2 weeks.

Massaman paste

MAKES 140g (about 7 tbsp)
PREP TIME: 15 mins
COOK TIME: 5 mins

1 tsp dried crushed chillies by Sainsbury's
1 tsp black peppercorns
1 tsp cumin seeds
1 tsp coriander seeds
1 tsp ground cinnamon
2 shallots, peeled and chopped
½ stalk fresh lemon grass, finely sliced
3 cloves garlic, crushed
2cm piece fresh ginger, peeled and chopped
½ tsp shrimp paste
½ tsp ground turmeric

1 Put the crushed chillies in a microwavable bowl with 5 tbsp water and microwave on medium

for 2 mins. Set aside and leave to soak for 20 mins.

2 Put the peppercorns, cumin and coriander seeds in a heavy-based frying pan and toast over a medium heat for 1-2 mins, until aromatic and lightly browned.

3 Pour the crushed chillies and soaking liquid into a mini food processor. Add the toasted spices and remaining ingredients; blend to a paste. Store in a clean sealed jar (see cook's tips) in the fridge for up to 2 weeks.

Cook's tips

For smooth pastes you'll need a mini food processor, stick blender or liquidiser. A standard-sized processer won't work.

If your processor isn't very powerful, use a pestle and mortar to crush seeds roughly before adding to the processor.

The seeds are the hottest part of the chilli, so add them to the paste if you want extra heat

To peel ginger, simply scrape away the skin with a knife or veg peeler.

Use the pastes immediately or see each recipe for storage information. Flavours will intensify if the paste is left for 1-2 days in the fridge.

Store pastes in screw-top jars. Wash the jars and lids in hot soapy water, rinse, then dry the jars in a medium oven (180°C, fan 160°C, gas 4) for 5 mins. Cool before adding the paste.

Freeze pastes for up to 1 month in ice cubes trays (each hole holds about ½ tbsp). Defrost before using.

Starters

HEAT
SERVES 4
PREP TIME 10 mins
COOK TIME 10 mins

Prawn tom yum

For a Thai menu from start to finish, serve this fresh and fragrant soup with our beef massaman (p90) and Thai coconut sorbet (p182)

1 clove garlic, chopped

2 lemon grass stalks, trimmed and chopped

2cm piece fresh ginger, peeled and chopped

4 fresh lime leaves, washed

3 green or red bird eye chillies, deseeded and 2 roughly chopped, 1 thinly sliced

200g pack pak choi by Sainsbury's, bases trimmed and leaves separated

2 x 180g packs fresh raw king prawns by Sainsbury's

2 tbsp palm sugar by Sainsbury's

3 tbsp fish sauce

5 tbsp lime juice

Handful fresh coriander leaves, roughly chopped, to garnish

1 Blitz the garlic, lemon grass, ginger, lime leaves and roughly chopped chillies in a mini food processor or blender to make a smooth paste.

2 Heat a large deep saucepan over a high heat, then add the paste and cook, stirring, for 1-2 mins, until fragrant. Add the pak choi and cook for a further min. Add 1 litre water, bring to the boil, then add the prawns. Cover and simmer for 4-5 mins, until the prawns are cooked through.

3 Take the pan off the heat and stir in the sugar, fish sauce and 3 tbsp of the lime juice. Taste and, if needed, adjust the flavouring with more sugar, fish sauce or the remaining lime juice. Season with freshly ground black pepper. Ladle into warm bowls and garnish with the fresh coriander and sliced chilli.

Per serving: 696kJ/165kcal (8%), 2.7g fat (4%), 0.6g saturates (3%), 6.7g sugars (7%), 2.92g salt (49%)

Cook's tip
You can replace the prawns with 1kg fresh mussels from the Sainsbury's fish counter. To prepare, scrub the mussels, pulling away any stringy 'beards' and discarding any that are open or remain open after tapping on a work surface. Simmer as above, until the mussels open, discarding any that remain closed.

HEAT
MAKES 12
PREP TIME 10 mins
COOK TIME
10-15 mins

Onion bhajis

This is one of the most popular Indian starters. Try serving with poppadums and our mango chutney (p161) and raita (p161), if you like

1 tsp cumin seeds
¼ tsp fennel seeds
75g plain four
50g rice flour
50g unsalted butter, melted
150ml sparkling water
1 clove garlic, finely chopped

1 green chilli, deseeded and finely chopped
Handful fresh coriander, roughly chopped
Small handful fresh mint leaves, finely chopped
2 medium onions, thinly sliced
Vegetable oil, for deep-frying

1   Bruise the cumin and fennel seeds with a pestle and mortar – you want them roughly crushed with some seeds still whole. Sift the flours into a large bowl, then add the melted butter and sparkling water to make a smooth batter with a consistency similar to double cream. Stir in the garlic, chilli, coriander, mint and the crushed spices. Add the onions and stir to coat in the batter.

2   Half fill a deep saucepan with vegetable oil for deep-frying and heat to 180°C or until a small spoonful of batter dropped into the hot oil sizzles and browns in 30 seconds.

3   Carefully drop 3 separate tbsp of the mixture into the hot oil. Stir the oil gently to prevent the bhajis sticking together and fry for 2-3 mins, turning occasionally, until evenly crisp and golden. Remove with a slotted spoon and drain on kitchen paper. Place the cooked bhajis on a baking sheet and keep warm in a low oven while cooking the remaining batter to make 12 bhajis in total.

Per serving (3 bhajis): 1875kJ/451kcal (19%), 34g fat (49%), 7.7g saturates (39%), 5.1g sugars (6%), <0.01g salt (<1%)

Cook's tip
Don't be tempted to cook more than 3 bhajis at a time as this will lower the oil temperature and, consequently, the bhajis will absorb more oil and become soggy instead of lovely and crisp.

Asian prawn omelette

This is a quick and easy starter to make. You can prepare the ingredients ahead of time and cook the omelettes as needed

6 medium eggs

1 tsp fish sauce

1 tbsp reduced salt soy sauce

¼ tsp ground white (or black) pepper

2 tbsp vegetable oil

225g pack Taste the Difference frozen raw jumbo king prawns, defrosted

75g sugar snap peas, sliced into 3 lengthways

3 spring onions, trimmed and finely sliced

Few sprigs of fresh coriander, leaves picked

1   Crack the eggs into a large bowl and whisk with the fish sauce, soy sauce and ground pepper.

2   Heat a shallow frying pan with 1 tbsp oil on a high heat; add half the prawns and sugar snap peas and cook for 2-3 mins until the prawns are pink and cooked through.

3   Turn the heat to low, pour in half the egg mixture and stir briefly. Scatter over just under half the spring onions and cook for 3 mins or until the eggs are just set. Gently fold the omelette in half, transfer to a warm plate and cover while you repeat with the remaining ingredients (wipe the pan with a piece of kitchen paper first).

4   To serve, scatter over the coriander and remaining spring onions, then cut each omelette in half.

Per serving (½ omelette): 905kJ/217cal (11%), 13.7g fat (20%), 2.9g saturates (15%), 1.7g sugars (2%), 1.84g salt (31%)

Cook's tip
To turn this into a main course, serve a whole omelette per person. Add a side dish of spiced carrot & radish salad (p165) to make this a substantial meal.

Sainsbury's
magazine
RECIPE

HEAT
MAKES 12
PREP TIME 20 mins
COOK TIME
about 10 mins

Indonesian prawn & sweetcorn cakes

If you want to extend your Indonesian theme to the main course, serve these gorgeously spicy little fritters before the beef rendang on p86

150g self raising flour
2 tsp hot chilli powder
1 tsp ground coriander
½ tsp ground cumin
2 medium eggs, beaten
198g tin naturally sweet sweetcorn by Sainsbury's, drained and rinsed
½ x 300g pack frozen basics cooked & peeled prawns, defrosted and chopped

1 clove garlic, crushed
1 large red chilli, finely chopped
1 small onion, finely chopped
Small handful fresh coriander, chopped, plus extra leaves to garnish
3-4 tbsp sunflower oil, for frying
Lime wedges, to serve
200g bag mixed salad leaves by Sainsbury's, to serve

1   Put the flour and spices in a bowl and stir to mix. Make a well in the centre and add the beaten eggs with 125ml cold water. Gradually whisk the liquid into the flour to form a smooth, thick batter.

2   Stir in the sweetcorn, prawns, garlic, chilli, onion and chopped coriander. Season to taste with freshly ground black pepper.

3   Heat 2 tbsp oil in a large frying pan and drop 4-6 large spoonfuls of batter into the pan. Fry over a medium heat for about 1½ mins on each side, until golden and cooked through. Remove and drain on kitchen paper. Cook the rest of the batter in the same way to make 12 in total, adding extra oil to the pan, if necessary.

4   Garnish with the extra coriander leaves. Serve with lime wedges and salad leaves. You can also serve with some sweet chilli sauce for dipping, if you like.

Per serving (3 cakes): 1435kJ/342kcal (17%), 14.2g fat (20%), 2.3g saturates (12%), 7.1g sugars (8%), 1.08g salt (18%)

Cook's tip
These fritters are great finger food for kids. To make them more child-friendly, just leave out the hot chilli powder and chopped fresh chilli.

HEAT
SERVES 4
PREP TIME 20 mins
COOK TIME
20-25 mins

Masala dosas

These feather-light pancakes hail from southern India, where they're eaten as either a street snack or for breakfast. Serve with raita (p161), if you like

600g potatoes, peeled and quartered
3 tbsp vegetable oil
2 tsp mustard seeds
3 fresh curry leaves, washed
1 onion, finely chopped
50g frozen peas, defrosted
2 green chillies, deseeded and finely chopped

3cm piece fresh ginger, peeled and finely chopped
¼ tsp ground turmeric
125g plain flour
125g gram flour by Sainsbury's
½ tsp bicarbonate of soda
Lime wedges, to serve

1   To make the filling, cook the potatoes in a large pan of lightly salted water for 10-15 mins, or until just tender, then drain thoroughly. Return to the pan and place over the heat for a further min to allow any excess moisture to evaporate. Transfer to a bowl and roughly crush with a fork or potato masher.

2   Meanwhile, heat 2 tbsp of the oil in a large frying pan or wok over a high heat. Fry the mustard seeds and curry leaves until the mustard seeds start to pop, then add the onion. Turn the heat down and fry for 3-4 mins, until the onion is soft. Add the peas, green chillies, ginger and turmeric and cook for a further min. Gently stir in the crushed potatoes.

3   To make the batter, tip both flours into a large bowl with the bicarbonate of soda. Season to taste, then whisk in about 350ml water to make a loose batter.

4   Heat a large shallow non-stick frying pan over a high heat and add a splash of the remaining oil. Use kitchen paper to spread the oil over the base and sides of the pan. Add a quarter of the batter and immediately swirl the pan so the batter coats the base and sides of the pan in a thin layer. Cook over a medium heat for about 1 min, until the pancake has just set and is golden underneath.

5   Spoon a quarter of the potato filling down one side of the pancake, then flip over the other side to enclose. Slide onto a plate (keep warm in a low oven) and repeat with the rest of the batter (adding extra oil as needed) and filling to make 4 dosas. Squeeze over lime juice to serve. You can also serve with raita (p161), if you like.

Per serving (1 masala dosa): 1917kJ/455kcal (23%), 10.8g fat (15%), 0.8g saturates (4%), 5.1g sugars (6%), 0.65g salt (11%)

HEAT
MAKES 16
PREP TIME 10 mins, plus resting
COOK TIME about 25 mins

Sweet potato pakoras

Vegetable fritters are a really popular snack in India - and you can make them with pretty much any veg you like. Serve with yogurt for dipping

125g gram flour by Sainsbury's
15g unsalted butter, melted
135ml sparkling water
¼ tsp ground nutmeg
½ tsp nigella seeds
5cm piece fresh ginger, peeled and grated
1 clove garlic, finely chopped

2 red chillies, deseeded and finely chopped
Vegetable oil, for frying
Small handful fresh coriander, finely chopped
1 large (about 300g) sweet potato, peeled and coarsely grated
Lime wedges, to serve

1   Sift the flour into a large bowl. Make a well in the centre, then whisk in the melted butter and enough sparkling water to make a smooth batter with a consistency slightly thicker than double cream. Stir in the nutmeg, nigella seeds, ginger, garlic and chillies, then season to taste. Leave to rest for 20 mins.

2   Half fill a wok or large deep frying pan with vegetable oil and heat to 180ºC, or until a cube of bread dropped in browns in about 30 seconds.

3   Stir the coriander and sweet potato into the batter and mix thoroughly. Carefully drop 3 tbsp of the mixture into the hot oil. Stir the oil gently to prevent the pakoras sticking together and cook for 1-2 mins on one side. Turn them over and cook for another 3-4 mins, turning occasionally, until evenly crisp and golden brown.

4   Remove with a slotted spoon and drain on kitchen paper. Repeat with the remaining batter to make about 16 pakoras in total. Serve warm with lime wedges to squeeze over. You can also serve with natural yogurt, if you like.

Per serving (4 pakoras): 1771kJ/426kcal (21%), 28.3g fat (40%), 3.7g saturates (19%), 5.7g sugars (6%), 0.11g salt (2%)

Variations
Spinach (palak) pakoras - replace the sweet potato with 250g roughly chopped young leaf spinach.
Potato (aloo) pakoras - replace the sweet potato with 2 baking potatoes, peeled and thickly sliced. Blanch the slices in boiling water for 1 min, then drain well before dipping each slice in the batter to coat. Fry the coated slices in the hot oil for 3-4 mins, turning once.

Meat samosas

These filo pastry treats are filled with a spicy mince and vegetable mixture. Try serving with our own mango chutney (p161) and raita (p161)

4 tbsp vegetable oil

1 onion, finely diced

5cm fresh ginger, peeled and grated

2 cloves garlic, finely chopped

½ tsp ground cinnamon

3-4 tbsp madras paste (p9) or 6-7 tbsp madras curry paste by Sainsbury's

250g pack 20% fat lamb mince by Sainsbury's or ½ x 500g pack 5% fat beef

mince by Sainsbury's (freeze the remainder to use another time)

1 medium potato, peeled and finely diced

40g frozen peas

Small handful fresh coriander, chopped

220g pack ready rolled filo pastry by Sainsbury's

2 tsp each nigella seeds and sesame seeds

1   Heat half the oil in a large pan over a medium heat and fry the onion for 5-6 mins, until softened. Add the ginger, garlic, cinnamon and madras paste, fry for a further min, then add the mince. Fry for a further 10-15 mins, stirring frequently, until browned and cooked through.

2   Meanwhile, cook the potato in a small pan of boiling water, until tender. Drain.

3   Stir the cooked diced potato and peas into the mince mixture and cook for a further 5 mins. Stir in the coriander and season to taste. Leave to cool.

4   Preheat the oven to 200ºC, fan 180ºC, gas 6. Lightly grease a large baking sheet.

5   Take 2 filo sheets and lay one on top of the other with the shortest edge in front of you. Brush lightly with some of the remaining oil and cut into 3 long strips. Put a spoonful of the mince mixture onto a corner of 1 strip. Fold the pastry and filling over at a right angle to make a triangular shape, then continue folding at right angles along the length of the strip to make a neat triangular parcel. Place on the baking sheet. Repeat to make 18 samosas in total from the remaining mince and filo pastry.

6   Lightly brush the samosas with any remaining oil and sprinkle with the nigella and sesame seeds. Bake for 20-25 mins, until crisp and golden. You can try serving with mango chutney (p161) and raita (p161), if you like.

Per samosa (made with beef): 449kJ/107kcal (5%), 5g fat (7%), 1g saturates (5%), 1g sugars (1%), 0.12g salt (2%)

HEAT
SERVES 4
PREP TIME 30
mins, plus resting
COOK TIME
15-20 mins

Prawn puris

Start your Indian feast in luxurious style with these mini deep-fried breads topped with a warm and aromatic prawn and tomato sauce

60g plain flour, plus extra for dusting
60g wholemeal flour
¼ tsp salt
2½ tbsp vegetable oil, plus extra for deep frying
2 whole cloves
3 shallots, thinly sliced
2 cloves garlic, crushed
½ tsp hot chilli powder
½ tsp ground cumin

½ tsp ground black pepper
1 tbsp malt vinegar
3 large tomatoes, skinned and chopped
1 tbsp tomato purée
Pinch of sugar
Few fresh curry leaves, washed
2 x 180g packs raw king prawns by Sainsbury's
Chopped fresh coriander, to garnish

1 To make the dough, mix the flours in a bowl with the salt. Drizzle over ½ tbsp oil, then stir in 90-100ml cold water and mix to a soft dough. Knead lightly for about 1 min, until smooth. If the dough is sticky, add a little more flour; if it's too dry to mix, sprinkle over a little more water. Wrap in cling film and rest for 30 mins.

2 Meanwhile, heat the remaining oil in a deep frying pan or wok and add the cloves. Fry over a high heat for a few seconds, then add the shallots and fry for 2-3 mins, until starting to brown. Add the garlic and fry for a further min. Reduce the heat, stir in the chilli powder, cumin, pepper and vinegar and cook for a few seconds.

3 Add the tomatoes, tomato purée, sugar, curry leaves and 6 tbsp water. Bring to the boil, then reduce the heat and stir in the prawns. Simmer for 5-6 mins, until the prawns are cooked through and the sauce has thickened slightly. Season to taste. Remove from the heat, cover and set aside.

4 Divide the dough into 8 and roll into balls. Dust a work surface with flour and roll out each ball to a thin 10cm circle. Half fill a wok or deep frying pan with oil and heat to 180°C or until a piece of the dough browns in 30 seconds. Slide the dough circles into the oil, 2 at a time, and deep-fry for a few seconds, turning occasionally, until golden and puffed up. Remove and drain on kitchen paper.

5 Gently reheat the prawn mixture for 1-2 mins. Serve 2 puris per person and top with the prawns. Garnish with chopped coriander.

Per serving (2 puris): 1248kJ/297kcal (15%), 9.6g fat (14%), 1.1g saturates (6%), 3.7g sugars (4%), 0.81g salt (14%)

HEAT
SERVES 4
PREP TIME 20 mins,
plus marinating
COOK TIME
10-15 mins

Lamb tikka kebabs

This classic recipe works just as well with cubed pork or chicken fillet.
Try serving with our home-made kachumber (p161) and raita (p161)

200g Greek style yogurt
2 tbsp tikka paste (p10) or 4 tbsp
tikka paste by Sainsbury's
2 tbsp lemon juice
411g pack diced lamb by Sainsbury's

1 large red onion, cut into chunks
1 large green pepper, deseeded and
cut into 2cm squares
Mint leaves, to garnish

1   Mix the yogurt, tikka paste and lemon juice in a non-metallic bowl. Add the lamb
    and stir to coat thoroughly in the marinade. Cover and leave in the fridge to
    marinate for at least 1 hour.

2   Preheat the grill to medium. Thread the marinated lamb, onion and pepper
    onto metal or pre-soaked wooden skewers (see cook's tip) and place on the
    wire rack of a grill pan. Spoon over any remaining marinade. Grill the kebabs
    for 10-15 mins, turning occasionally, until the lamb is cooked and lightly charred
    in places. Garnish with mint leaves to serve. You can also trying serving with raita
    (p161) and kachumber (p161), if you like.

Per serving: 1641kJ/394kcal (20%), 25.7g fat (37%), 12.6g saturates (63%),
6.2g sugars (7%), 0.32g salt (5%)

Cook's tip
If you're using wooden skewers instead of metal ones,
soak them in cold water for 15 mins before loading
with the lamb and vegetables to stop them burning.
The tips may still catch under a hot grill, so wrap small
pieces of foil around the tips to stop this happening.

Chicken

Jungle curry	34
Chicken korma	36
Chicken jalfrezi	38
Lassi	38
Penang curry	40
Sticky rice	40
Chicken katsu curry	42
Chicken dupiaza	44
Balinese chicken	46
South Indian curry	48
Nyonya curry	50
Chicken dhansak	52
Caribbean chicken curry	54
Vietnamese chicken	56
Chicken vindaloo	58
Chicken karahi	60
Chicken tikka masala	62
Tandoori chicken	64
Butter chicken	66

HEAT 〝〝
SERVES 4
PREP TIME 10 mins
COOK TIME 20 mins
2 of 5
A-DAY

Jungle curry

Heat and flavour combine in this dish to produce a memorable Thai curry experience. Ideal for using up leftover roast turkey or chicken

1 tbsp vegetable oil
1 tbsp fish sauce
1 tsp light brown soft sugar
200g pack Sainsbury's baby aubergines, trimmed and cut into 2cm chunks
100g new potatoes, quartered
225g tin bamboo shoots, drained and rinsed
200g cooked turkey or chicken, shredded
200g pack baby corn & mange tout by Sainsbury's
250g basmati rice, cooked, to serve

FOR THE CURRY PASTE
1-2 red or green bird eye chillies, deseeded and roughly chopped
2cm piece fresh ginger, peeled and chopped
2 fresh lemon grass stalks, chopped
4 shallots, chopped
4 cloves garlic
4 dried kaffir lime leaves, washed
½ tsp shrimp paste
1 tbsp groundnut oil

1   Put all the curry paste ingredients in a food processor with 3 tbsp water and process until smooth. You can make the curry paste a few hours ahead, then cover and chill until you're ready to cook.

2   Heat the oil in a heavy-based pan. Add the curry paste and stir-fry for 2 mins. Reduce the heat to medium and add 500ml water. Stir well.

3   Add the fish sauce and sugar. Cook for 2 mins. Add the aubergines and potatoes, and cook for 6-8 mins, or until they start to soften. Add the bamboo shoots and cooked turkey or chicken and simmer for 5 mins.

4   Add the baby corn and mange tout, and simmer for a further 3-4 mins until the vegetables are tender. Serve with the cooked basmati rice.

Per serving of curry with rice: 1701kJ/403kcal (20%), 6.9g fat (10%), 1.1g saturates (6%), 4.8g sugars (5%), 1.13g salt (19%)

Sainsbury's
magazine
RECIPE

HEAT
SERVES 4
PREP TIME 20mins
COOK TIME 25 mins

Chicken korma

With its restrained spices and creamy sauce, a chicken korma
is a popular choice for those who prefer a milder curry

50g unsalted cashew nuts

1 tbsp vegetable oil

3 whole cloves

1 cinnamon stick

2 onions, finely chopped

3 cloves garlic, finely chopped

460g pack British chicken thigh fillets by
Sainsbury's, cut into chunks

2 tbsp korma paste (p9), or 5 tbsp
korma paste by Sainsbury's

150g Greek-style natural yogurt

4 tbsp double cream

Fresh coriander leaves, chopped,
to garnish (optional)

1   Put the cashew nuts in a mini food processor with 2 tbsp water and process to
a coarse paste. Set aside.

2   Heat the oil in a large deep frying pan over a medium heat and fry the cloves
and cinnamon stick for 1-2 mins until aromatic. Add the onions and garlic and
fry for 4-5 mins until softened. Add the chicken and fry over a high heat, stirring
frequently, for 5 mins or until no longer pink on the outside. Add the korma
paste and stir to coat the chicken, then cook for a further min.

3   Reduce the heat and stir in the cashew nut paste, yogurt and double cream.
Simmer gently for 10-12 mins, stirring occasionally, until the chicken is cooked
through with no pink colour remaining and the sauce is thick and creamy. Season
to taste. Garnish with fresh coriander leaves. We suggest you try serving this
with jeera rice (p156).

Per serving of curry without rice: 2046kJ/492kcal (25%), 33.3g fat (48%),
12.2g saturates (61%), 8g sugars (9%), 0.21g salt (4%)

Drink suggestion
A glass of zesty, dry white wine will go very nicely with
this curry – try Taste the Difference Coolwater Bay
Sauvignon Blanc from New Zealand.

Chicken jalfrezi

Fresh tomatoes, peppers and chicken in a deliciously spicy sauce. We love it! Serve with naan bread (p158) to scoop up all that lovely hot curry sauce

1 tbsp sunflower oil
1 large onion, roughly chopped
2 red chillies, deseeded and thinly sliced
6 tbsp jalfrezi paste (p8) or
5 tbsp shop-bought jalfrezi paste

615g pack chicken thigh fillets by Sainsbury's, cut into chunks
1 large red pepper and 1 large yellow pepper, deseeded and cut into chunks
2 large tomatoes, chopped
Handful fresh coriander, chopped

1   Heat the oil in a large deep frying pan and fry the onion over a medium heat for 5 mins until beginning to soften. Add the chillies and fry for a further min. Stir in the jalfrezi paste and cook, stirring, for 1-2 mins.

2   Add the chicken and cook over a high heat for 2-3 mins until no longer pink on the outside. Stir in 250ml water and the peppers and tomatoes. Bring to the boil, then reduce the heat to a simmer and cook for 20 mins, stirring occasionally, until the chicken is tender and cooked through with no pink colour remaining and the sauce has thickened.

3   Season to taste and stir in most of the chopped coriander, then garnish with the remaining coriander. Serve with naan bread (p158), if you like, and while you're eating this curry, you may want to cool down the heat with a lassi (see below).

Per serving of curry without naan: 1643kJ/393kcal (20%), 20.2g fat (29%), 4.9g saturates (25%), 9.5g sugars (11%), 0.22g salt (4%)

Lassi

Put 400g fresh mango pieces in a large blender with 500ml low-fat natural yogurt, the leaves from 4 sprigs of fresh mint and 200ml water. Whizz until smooth, pour into glasses and decorate with some extra chopped fresh mango and mint.

Serves 4 Prep time: 5 mins
Per drink: 647kJ/153kcal (8%), 2.1g fat (3%), 1.2g saturates (6%), 24.1g sugars (27%), <0.01g salt (less than 1%)

Penang curry

This curry comes with plenty of fresh flavours and a good hit of heat

2 tbsp vegetable oil
400ml tin coconut milk
500g pack Freedom Food British chicken breast fillets by Sainsbury's, cut into strips
Juice of ½ lime
Thinly sliced red chilli, to garnish

FOR THE PASTE
3 dried red chillies
2 shallots, chopped
3 cloves garlic, chopped
2 tsp galangal paste by Sainsbury's

2 fresh kaffir lime leaves, chopped, plus extra shredded to garnish
1 lemon grass stalk, trimmed and chopped
2 tbsp chopped fresh coriander stalks
1 tbsp soy sauce
1 tbsp fish sauce
3 tbsp tomato purée
1 tsp shrimp paste
2 tsp ground coriander
2 tsp ground cumin
2 tsp paprika

1   For the paste, soak the chillies in 4 tbsp boiling water for 15 mins. Drain (remove the seeds) and blend in a processor with the remaining paste ingredients and 2 tbsp cold water. Heat the oil in a large frying pan and add the paste. Fry, stirring, for 2-3 mins, until the oil starts to separate. Gradually stir in the coconut milk.

2   Add the chicken and simmer for 20 mins, until cooked through with no pink colour remaining. Stir in the lime juice. Garnish with the lime leaves and sliced red chilli, then ladle into bowls and serve with sticky rice (below), if you like.

Per serving of curry without rice: 1736kJ/415kcal (21%), 23.2g fat (33%), 14.3g saturates (72%), 4.8g sugars (5%), 1.78g salt (30%)

Sticky rice

Soak 250g Thai sticky rice by Sainsbury's in cold water for 15 mins. Drain. Pour 450ml water into a pan; stir in the rice, 1 tsp caster sugar and a pinch of salt. Boil, reduce the heat, cover and simmer for 12-14 mins, until the water is absorbed. Garnish with 1 tbsp toasted sesame seeds.

Serves 4 Prep time: 5 mins Cook time: 12-14 mins

Per serving: 1021kJ/241kcal (12%), 2.5g fat (4%), 0.4g saturates (2%), 1.4g sugars (2%), <0.01g salt (<1%)

Chicken katsu curry

This classic Japanese dish of crispy chicken in a rich curry sauce is served with a delicious pickle of cucumber, carrot and radish

Vegetable oil for deep-frying, plus extra 2 tbsp
1 onion, finely chopped
1 clove garlic, finely chopped
2cm piece fresh ginger, peeled and grated
1 tbsp medium curry powder by Sainsbury's
6 tbsp plain flour
500ml chicken stock, made with 1 stock cube
1½ tbsp soy sauce
2 tsp mirin
2 tsp clear honey
4 chicken breast fillets
2 medium eggs, beaten

100g panko breadcrumbs
2 spring onions, trimmed and shredded, to garnish

FOR THE PICKLE
50ml rice wine vinegar
1 tbsp caster sugar
½ cucumber, halved, deseeded and sliced
1 carrot, peeled and sliced into ribbons
75g radishes, trimmed and thinly sliced
2cm piece fresh ginger, peeled and very thinly sliced

1 For the pickle, bring the vinegar, sugar and 1 tbsp water to the boil in a pan, then simmer, stirring, until the sugar dissolves. Put the vegetables in a large bowl and pour over the vinegar. Stir well and set aside to cool. Cover and chill in the fridge.

2 Heat the extra 2 tbsp vegetable oil in a large pan and cook the onion over a gentle heat for 10 mins, adding in the garlic and ginger for the final 1 min. Stir in the curry powder and 3 tbsp plain flour and cook for 1 further min.

3 Add the chicken stock, a little at a time, stirring constantly. Bring to a simmer and cook for 10 mins. Stir in the soy sauce, mirin and honey. Transfer to a blender, allow to cool a little and blitz to a purée. Pour back into the pan and cover.

4 Meanwhile, put the chicken breasts between cling film and bash with a rolling pin to an even thickness. Cover each breast with the remaining flour, dip in the egg, then roll in the panko breadcrumbs to fully cover. Chill in the fridge for 15 mins.

5 Meanwhile, fill a large pan a third full with the oil. Heat until hot enough to brown a cube of bread in 30 seconds. Fry 2 chicken breasts at a time for 4-5 mins until cooked through with no pink colour remaining. Remove and serve with the sauce and pickle. Garnish with spring onions. Serve with sticky rice (p40), if you like.

Per serving of curry without rice: 3116kJ/744kcal (37%), 34.6g fat (49%), 3.9g saturates (20%), 14.8g sugars (16%), 2.41g salt (40%)

Chicken dupiaza

A mildly spiced onion and tomato-based curry that's delicious with naan bread (p158) and bhindi masala recipe (p165) on the side

3 tbsp vegetable oil

2 large onions, half of 1 onion finely chopped and the rest roughly chopped

2 cloves garlic, crushed

3cm piece fresh ginger, peeled and grated

2 tsp ground coriander

1 tsp ground cumin

½ tsp turmeric

1½ tsp hot chilli powder

500g pack chicken breast fillets by Sainsbury's, cut into large chunks

230g tin chopped tomatoes by Sainsbury's

300ml chicken stock made with 1 stock cube

1 tsp garam masala

Large handful fresh coriander, chopped

1   Heat 1 tbsp of the oil in a large deep frying pan over a high heat and fry the roughly chopped onions for 5 mins until just beginning to soften and brown. Remove with a slotted spoon and set aside.

2   Add the rest of the oil to the pan and add the finely chopped onion, garlic and ginger. Fry over a medium heat, stirring occasionally, for 5 mins then stir in the coriander, cumin, turmeric and chilli powder and cook for a further 1-2 mins.

3   Add the chicken and fry over a high heat, stirring continuously, for 4-5 mins, or until no longer pink on the outside. Return the fried onions to the pan and add the tomatoes and stock. Season to taste with freshly ground black pepper. Simmer for 15-20 mins, stirring occasionally, until the chicken is cooked through with no pink colour remaining and the sauce has reduced and thickened.

4   Stir in the garam masala and most of the chopped coriander and cook for a further min. Serve garnished with the remaining coriander. This curry goes really well with naan bread (p158) and bhindi masala (p165).

Per serving of curry without accompaniments: 1298kJ/309kcal (16%), 11.2g fat (16%), 1.5g saturates (8%), 6.7g sugars (7.1%), 1.42g salt (24%)

Balinese chicken

The unmistakable flavours of Indonesia run through this fragrant curry with its rich cashew and coconut sauce. Serve with sticky rice (p40)

1 large onion, chopped

3 cloves garlic, crushed

3cm piece fresh ginger, peeled and grated

2 red chillies, deseeded and chopped, plus extra sliced to garnish

1 lemon grass stalk, trimmed and finely chopped

Juice of 1 large lime

1 tbsp light soy sauce

2 tsp ground coriander

1 tsp ground turmeric

100g unsalted cashew nuts

1½ tbsp vegetable oil

1 tbsp palm sugar

¼ tsp salt

4 chicken leg portions, skin removed

400ml tin reduced fat coconut milk

1 Put the onion, garlic, ginger, chillies and lemon grass in a food processor with the lime juice, soy sauce, coriander and turmeric. Add 75g of the cashew nuts. Process for about 30 seconds to make a coarse paste.

2 Heat the oil in a large casserole over a high heat and fry the remaining cashew nuts for a few secs until just golden. Remove with a slotted spoon and drain on kitchen paper. Roughly chop, then set aside.

3 Add the onion and cashew nut paste to the casserole with the palm sugar. Reduce the heat to low and cook for about 10 mins, stirring all the time, until the paste is beginning to turn golden and caramelise.

4 Add the chicken portions and stir to coat in the paste. Cook for 5 mins, turning, until no longer pink on the outside. Pour in the coconut milk and bring to the boil. Reduce the heat and cover and simmer for 30 mins, stirring occasionally.

5 Uncover the casserole and simmer for a further 10-15 mins, until the chicken is cooked through with no pink colour remaining and the sauce has thickened slightly. Season to taste.

6 Garnish the chicken with the fried cashew nuts and serve with extra sliced red chilli on the side. Why not try serving this with sticky rice (p40).

Per serving of curry without rice: 1927kJ/461kcal (23%), 26.2g fat (37%), 9.7g saturates (49%), 8.5g sugars (9%), 0.78g salt (13%)

HEAT

SERVES 4
PREP TIME 20 mins
COOK TIME
50-55 mins

1 of 5
A-DAY

South Indian curry

Everyone will love this mild curry as it's both easy to make
and perfect for those who have a low chilli heat tolerance!

2 tbsp vegetable oil	plus extra to garnish (optional)
1 tsp mustard seeds	2 tsp ground coriander
3 onions, halved and thinly sliced	½ tsp ground turmeric
Few fresh curry leaves, washed	1½ tsp garam masala
4cm piece fresh ginger, peeled and grated	¼ tsp black pepper
4 cloves garlic, crushed	8 chicken thighs, bone-in, skin removed
1 green chilli, deseeded and thinly sliced,	1 tsp tamarind paste

1   Heat the oil in a large deep frying pan over a high heat. Add the mustard seeds
    and cook for a few seconds until they start to pop. Stir in the onions and fry over
    a medium heat, stirring frequently for 5 mins. Add the curry leaves, ginger, garlic
    and chilli and fry for a further 5 mins until the onions are soft and golden.

2   Stir in the coriander, turmeric, garam masala and black pepper and fry for a
    further min, then add the chicken thighs and turn to coat in the onion mixture.
    Pour in 400ml cold water and bring to the boil. Reduce the heat, cover and
    simmer for 30 mins, stirring occasionally.

3   Blend the tamarind paste with 1 tbsp hot water and stir into the curry. Simmer,
    uncovered, for a further 10-15 mins until the sauce has reduced slightly and
    the chicken is cooked through with no pink colour remaining. Season to taste
    and serve. This is great served with jeera rice (p156) and a side of cabbage
    poiyal (p162).

Per serving of curry without rice and side dish: 1717kJ/411kcal (21%), 22.3g fat
(32%), 4.9g saturates (25%), 7.6g sugars (8%), 0.21g salt (4%)

Cook's tip
If you prefer serving this curry without rice, add
250g quartered new potatoes with the chicken thighs
and 200g young spinach leaves to the curry at the end
of the cooking time, stirring until just wilted.

HEAT
SERVES 4
PREP TIME 20 mins, plus soaking
COOK TIME 45 mins

Nyonya curry

If you're in the mood for something hot, then this Malaysian curry will hit the spot. Team it with sticky rice (p40), if you like

3 dried red chillies
4 shallots, chopped
3 cloves garlic, chopped
15g shrimp paste
1 tbsp ground coriander
1 tsp ground cumin
1 tsp ground turmeric
2 tbsp vegetable oil
1 cinnamon stick

3 cloves
1 whole star anise
500g pack Freedom Food British chicken breast fillets by Sainsbury's, cut into chunks
500g potatoes, peeled and cut into chunks
400ml tin reduced fat coconut milk
1 tsp palm sugar
50g creamed coconut
Juice of ½ lime

1   Soak the dried red chillies in 4 tbsp boiling water for 15 mins. Drain (removing the seeds) and put in a food processor with the shallots, garlic, shrimp paste, coriander, cumin and turmeric. Add 2 tbsp water and process to a coarse paste.

2   Heat the oil in a large deep frying pan and add the cinnamon stick, cloves and star anise. Fry over a high heat for 1-2 mins until sizzling, then add the paste and fry, over a medium heat, for 5-6 mins, stirring all the time.

3   Add the chicken and cook, stirring, for 2 mins until no longer pink on the outside. Add the potatoes and stir to coat in the spice paste. Pour in the coconut milk and add the palm sugar. Bring to the boil, then reduce the heat, cover and simmer for 30 mins, stirring occasionally until the chicken is cooked through with no pink colour remaining and the potatoes are tender.

4   Stir in the creamed coconut and simmer, uncovered, for a further few mins until it has dissolved into the sauce. Stir in the lime juice to serve. This dish is great served with sticky rice (p40).

Per serving of curry without rice: 2142kJ/511kcal (26%), 23.4g fat (33%), 14.7g saturates (74%), 4.1g sugars (5%), 1.22g salt (20%)

Drink suggestion
Taste the Difference American Pale Ale is a great choice to serve with this spicy dish.

HEAT
SERVES 4
PREP TIME 20 mins, plus soaking
COOK TIME about 1 hour

Chicken dhansak

We suggest serving this well-loved lentil-based chicken curry with home-made chapattis (p159) and spicy basmati rice (p157)

200g red lentils

1 large onion, chopped

2 cloves garlic, chopped

3cm piece fresh ginger, peeled and chopped

2 tbsp vegetable oil

3 tbsp balti paste (p9), or 6 tbsp balti paste by Sainsbury's

4 chicken thighs, skin removed

4 chicken drumsticks, skin removed

450ml chicken stock made with 1 stock cube

3 large tomatoes, peeled and chopped

4 baby aubergines, trimmed and halved lengthways

Handful fresh coriander, roughly chopped

---

1 Rinse the red lentils in cold water, then soak in a bowl of cold water for 10 mins.

2 Meanwhile, put the onion, garlic and ginger in a food processor and process for a few seconds until finely minced. Heat the oil in a large casserole and add the minced mixture. Fry for 7-8 mins until starting to brown, then stir in the balti paste and cook for a further 1-2 mins, stirring all the time.

3 Add the chicken and fry over a medium heat for 10 mins, turning frequently. Drain the lentils and add to the casserole with the stock. Bring to the boil, then reduce to a simmer, cover and cook for 25 mins, stirring occasionally.

4 Add the tomatoes and aubergines and cook, uncovered, for 15-20 mins until the chicken is cooked through with no pink colour remaining, the aubergines are tender and the lentils have broken down to create a thick sauce.

5 Stir in most of the coriander and season to taste. Sprinkle over the remaining coriander to garnish. This goes really well with chapattis (p159) and our spicy basmati rice with coriander & mint (p157).

Per serving of curry without rice and chapattis: 1408kJ/336kcal (17%), 14.8g fat (21%), 3.1g saturates (16%), 5.3g sugars (6%), 1.26g salt (21%)

Cook's tip
To peel the tomatoes, score a cross in the top of each one with a knife. Cover with boiling water and leave for 1-2 mins. Drain, then cover with cold water and leave for 1 min. Drain and the skins should peel away easily.

Caribbean chicken curry

Spicy jerk paste, tomatoes and creamy coconut milk combine to delicious effect in this Caribbean-inspired curry

2 tbsp vegetable oil	2 tbsp red wine vinegar
8 chicken thighs	390g carton chopped tomatoes
1 onion, finely chopped	by Sainsbury's
3 garlic cloves, finely chopped	400ml tin reduced-fat coconut milk
3cm piece fresh ginger, peeled and finely chopped	600g sweet potatoes, peeled and cut into cubes
2 tbsp spicy jerk paste by Sainsbury's	1 red pepper, deseeded and sliced
4 sprigs fresh thyme, leaves picked	410g tin mixed pulses in water by Sainsbury's,
2 bird eye chillies, deseeded and chopped	drained and rinsed

1   Heat 1 tbsp of the oil in a large shallow casserole, over a medium heat, and cook the chicken thighs, skin-side down for 3-4 mins, until golden then turn over and cook for a further 4-5 mins. Remove and set aside.

2   Heat the remaining oil in the casserole and cook the onion for 10 mins, adding in the garlic and ginger for the last min. Stir in the jerk paste, thyme leaves and chillies and cook for a further 2 mins.

3   Preheat the oven to 180°C, fan 160°C, gas 4. Add the vinegar, tomatoes, coconut milk, sweet potato, pepper and pulses to the onion mix and season to taste. Gently bring to the boil, then reduce the heat and simmer for 2-3 mins. Remove from the heat.

4   Return the chicken thighs to the casserole skin-side up, place in the oven and cook, uncovered, for 35-45 mins until cooked through with no pink colour remaining.

Per serving: 3120kJ/746kcal (37%), 35.4g fat (51%), 12.4g saturates (62%), 19.2g sugars (21%), 0.64g salt (11%)

Drink suggestion
Enjoy more Caribbean flavours by teaming this with Taste the Difference alcoholic ginger beer.

HEAD
SERVES 4
PREP TIME
15-20 mins
COOK TIME 1 hour
20 mins

Vietnamese chicken

Whole chicken is so flavoursome when cooked in this fragrant coconut-based sauce. Plenty of added veg makes it an all-in-one meal

1 tbsp vegetable oil
5 shallots, sliced
2 fresh lemon grass stalks, trimmed, bruised and halved lengthways
3cm piece fresh ginger, peeled and finely chopped
3 cloves garlic, finely chopped
2 bird eye chillies, deseeded and sliced
2 tbsp madras curry paste (p9), or
4 tbsp madras paste by Sainsbury's
600ml chicken stock, made with 1 stock cube
400ml tin reduced fat coconut milk

1.35kg whole chicken
4 fresh kaffir lime leaves, washed
2 whole star anise
600g sweet potatoes, peeled and cut into 2cm cubes
2 tbsp fish sauce
1 tsp light brown soft sugar
100g okra, chopped
200g pack trimmed mange tout by Sainsbury's
Juice of 2 limes

1   Heat the oil in a large deep casserole over a medium heat and cook the shallots for 4-5 mins. Stir in the lemon grass, ginger, garlic and half the chillies and cook for a further 2-3 mins. Add in the madras curry paste and cook for 1-2 mins, until fragrant, then stir in the chicken stock and coconut milk. Bring to the boil, then turn down to a very gentle simmer and cook for 5 mins.

2   Preheat the oven to 190ºC, fan 170ºC, gas 5. Stir the stock mix, then gently lower the whole chicken into the casserole. Add the kaffir lime leaves and star anise. Place into the oven and cook for 45 mins, uncovered, until the juices of the chicken run clear when the thickest part of the leg is pierced with a knife and no pink colour remains.

3   Remove the chicken from the casserole and leave to rest on a carving board, covered in foil.

4   Place the casserole on a medium heat and add the sweet potato, fish sauce and brown sugar. Bring to a gentle simmer and cook for 15 mins. Stir in the okra and mange tout and cook for a further 2-3 mins, until the vegetables are just tender. Stir in the lime juice. Serve the chicken sliced with the curried vegetables.

Per serving: 2765kJ/660kcal (33%), 28.1g fat (40%), 11.5g saturates (58%), 14.7g sugars (16%), 3.06g salt (51%)

HEAT)))
SERVES 4
PREP TIME 20-25 mins, plus 1 hour marinating
COOK TIME 50 mins

Chicken vindaloo

Vindaloo reputedly started out as Portuguese dish that was exported to its colony in Goa where it was supercharged into this fiery curry

3 tbsp red wine vinegar

3cm piece fresh ginger, peeled and finely chopped

2 dried chillies, thickly sliced and soaked in 1 tbsp boiling water to rehydrate

1 tsp ground cumin

1 tsp garam masala

3 tbsp tandoori paste (p9), or 6 tbsp shop-bought tandoori paste

850g pack chicken thighs and drumsticks by Sainsbury's, each piece slashed in 3 places

2 tbsp vegetable oil

1 onion, finely chopped

1-2 bird eye chillies, finely chopped

1 tsp mustard seeds

5 garlic cloves, finely chopped

1 cinnamon stick

2 tsp coriander seeds

½ tsp turmeric

2 tbsp tomato purée

390g carton chopped tomatoes by Sainsbury's

2 tsp light brown soft sugar

1   In a food processor, whizz together 2 tbsp of the vinegar with the ginger, dried chillies, cumin, garam masala and 1 tbsp tandoori paste. When you have a smooth paste, tip it over the chicken thighs and drumsticks and massage it into the flesh. Leave for 1 hour to marinate.

2   Preheat the oven to 200ºC, fan 180ºC, gas 6. Put the chicken into a non-stick baking dish and cook for 30 mins, until the skin is crisp and the chicken is cooked through with no pink colour remaining.

3   Meanwhile, heat the oil in a large pan and cook the onion for 5 mins until softened. Add the chilli, mustard seeds, garlic, cinnamon stick, coriander seeds and turmeric, and cook, stirring, for 2 mins. Stir in the remaining tandoori paste with the tomato purée and cook for 2-3 mins.

4   Add the tomatoes, sugar, remaining vinegar and 400ml water. Bring to a gentle simmer, season to taste and cook for 5-10 mins. Add the roasted chicken pieces and cook for 15-20 mins. Try serving this with saffron rice (p157), if you like.

Per serving of curry without rice: 1331kJ/318kcal (16%), 15.7g fat (22%), 2.8g saturates (14%), 8.5g sugars (9%), 0.15g salt (3%)

HEAT 🌶🌶🌶
SERVES 4
PREP TIME 20
mins, plus 2-3 hours
marinating
COOK TIME 35 mins

Chicken karahi

A karahi is the traditional circular steel pot used for cooking in India. A deep frying pan works just as well for cooking up this spicy chicken curry

8 skinless and boneless chicken thigh fillets

3 cloves garlic, crushed

3cm piece fresh ginger, peeled and grated

1 tbsp lemon juice

½ tsp ground turmeric

2 tsp hot chilli powder

2 tbsp vegetable oil

1 cinnamon stick

4 cardamom pods, lightly crushed

1 onion, roughly chopped

390g carton chopped tomatoes by Sainsbury's

1 tsp ground cumin

2 tsp ground coriander

2 green chillies, deseeded and quartered lengthways

1 green pepper, deseeded and diced

Handful fresh coriander, chopped

1 tsp garam masala

Fresh mint leaves, to garnish

1   Put the chicken fillets in a large non-metallic bowl and add the garlic, ginger, lemon juice, turmeric and chilli powder, stir well to coat the chicken. Cover and put in the fridge to marinate for 2-3 hours.

2   Heat the oil in a large deep frying pan over a high heat, add the cinnamon stick and cardamom pods and fry for 1-2 mins to release their aroma. Add the onion and fry over a medium heat, stirring, for 6-7 mins until softened and golden.

3   Add the marinated chicken to the pan and stir-fry over a high heat until it's no longer pink on the outside. Stir in the tomatoes, cumin, coriander, chillies, green pepper and 3 tbsp water. Season to taste.

4   Bring to the boil, then cover and reduce to a simmer for 20 mins, stirring occasionally, until the chicken is tender and cooked through with no pink colour remaining and the sauce has reduced and thickened. Stir in the coriander and garam masala and cook for a further min. Serve garnished with fresh mint leaves. This curry works really well with pilau rice (p157).

Per serving of curry without rice: 1695kJ/406kcal (20%), 22.7g fat (32%), 4.9g saturates (25%), 6.3g sugars (7%), 0.24g salt (4%)

HEAT
SERVES 4
PREP TIME 20 mins, plus at least 3-4 hours marinating
COOK TIME 45 mins

Chicken tikka masala

Consistently hailed as one of Britain's favourite dishes, this tikka masala is easy to make and works a treat with a serving of jeera rice (p156)

500g pack Freedom Food British chicken breast fillets by Sainsbury's, cut into chunks
2 tbsp lemon juice
4 tbsp tikka paste (p10), or 6 tbsp tikka paste by Sainsbury's

FOR THE MASALA SAUCE
2 tbsp vegetable oil
2 onions, finely sliced
2 cloves garlic, crushed

3cm piece fresh ginger, peeled and grated
1 tsp ground coriander
1 tsp paprika
½ tsp ground turmeric
½ tsp hot chilli powder
4 tbsp low fat natural yogurt
2 tbsp tomato purée
4 tbsp single cream
¼ tsp garam masala
Small handful fresh coriander leaves

1   Put the chicken in a shallow, non-metallic bowl, add the lemon juice and season. Cover and leave at room temperature for 20 mins.

2   Stir in the tikka paste and mix to coat all the chicken pieces thoroughly with the paste. Cover and leave to marinate in the fridge for 3-4 hours (or overnight).

3   To make the masala sauce, heat the oil in a large deep frying pan over a high heat. Add the onions and fry for 6-7 mins until soft and golden, then add the garlic and ginger and fry for a further 1-2 mins.

4   Add the coriander, paprika, turmeric and chilli powder and cook for 30 seconds, then gradually stir in the yogurt. Stir in 350ml water and the purée, and season to taste. Cover and simmer for 25-30 mins, stirring occasionally, until the sauce has thickened. Stir in the cream and garam masala, and simmer until thickened.

5   While the sauce is cooking, preheat the grill to medium-high and thread the marinated chicken onto 2-3 long metal skewers then place on a baking tray. Cook the skewers under a medium-hot grill for 15-20 mins, turning occasionally, until the chicken is cooked through with no pink colour remaining.

6   Slide the chicken off the skewers into the sauce and stir to coat. Heat through for 1 min. Garnish with coriander leaves and serve with jeera rice (p156), if you like.

Per serving of curry without rice: 1387kJ/330kcal (17%), 12.5g fat (18%), 3.6g saturates (18%), 8.2g sugars (9%), 0.2g salt (3%)

HEAT
SERVES 4
PREP TIME 10 mins,
plus at least 3-4
hours marinating
COOK TIME
35-40 mins

Tandoori chicken

Tandoori chicken is traditionally cooked in a clay oven over charcoal.
We've cooked ours in a conventional oven but you could also
try cooking this on the barbecue to get the chargrilled flavour

4 chicken leg portions (about 1.2kg in total),
skin removed and excess fat removed
6 tbsp tandoori paste (p9) or 6 tbsp
shop-bought tandoori paste

6 tbsp low fat natural yogurt
Lime halves, to garnish

1 Slash each chicken portion 3-4 times and place in a shallow non-metallic dish.

2 Mix together the tandoori paste and yogurt, then spoon over the chicken.
   Turn the chicken to coat completely in the marinade, rubbing it into the slashed
   flesh. Cover and leave to marinate in the fridge for 3-4 hours (or overnight, see
   cook's tip).

3 Preheat the oven to 220ºC, fan 200ºC, gas 7. Put the marinated chicken on
   a metal rack set over a roasting tin. Spoon over any marinade left in the bowl.
   Cook for 15 mins, then reduce the oven temperature to 200ºC, fan 180ºC, gas
   6 and cook for a further 20-25 mins, until the chicken is cooked through with no
   pink colour remaining.

4 Serve the chicken garnished with lime halves. This tastes really great with raita
   (p161) and kachumber (p161).

Per serving of chicken without raita and kachumber: 917kJ/218cal (11%), 7.7g fat
(11%), 1.9g saturates (10%), 1.8g sugars (2%), 0.35g salt (6%)

Cook's tip
Leaving the chicken to marinate overnight will help
to tenderise the flesh and add lots of extra flavour.

HEAT
SERVES 4
PREP TIME 20 mins, plus at least 4 hours marinating
COOK TIME 45 mins

Butter chicken

This creamy chicken curry has a mild and sweet flavour so add a little chopped red chilli if you want to give it a boost of fiery heat

500g pack Freedom Food British chicken breast fillets by Sainsbury's, cut into chunks
3 tbsp tikka paste (p10), or 6 tbsp tikka paste by Sainsbury's
3 tbsp low-fat natural yogurt
1 small onion, chopped
2 cloves garlic, crushed
4cm piece fresh ginger, peeled and grated
40g unsalted butter
1 tsp hot chilli powder

1 tsp ground cumin
1½ tsp ground coriander
1½ tsp garam masala
1 tsp ground turmeric
500g carton passata by Sainsbury's
2 tsp lemon juice
1 tsp sugar
¼ tsp salt
200ml single cream
Fresh coriander leaves, to garnish

1 Put the chicken in a non-metallic bowl. Add the tikka paste and yogurt and mix well to coat. Cover and marinate in the fridge for 4 hours (or overnight).

2 Preheat the oven to 180ºC, fan 160ºC, gas 4. Put the marinated chicken pieces on a wire rack set over a baking tray. Cook for 10 mins, then turn over and cook for a further 10-15 mins, or until just cooked through with no pink colour remaining.

3 Meanwhile, put the onion, garlic and ginger in a food processor and process for a few seconds until finely minced. Heat half the butter in a large, deep frying pan and fry the minced onion mixture over a medium heat for 10-12 mins, stirring frequently, until softened and golden. Add all the spices and fry for a further 2-3 mins.

4 Stir in the passata, lemon juice, sugar and salt, and simmer gently for 15 mins. Stir in the remaining butter and nearly all the cream, and simmer for 1-2 mins until the butter has melted. Add the cooked chicken pieces to the pan and stir gently to coat in the sauce. Season to taste. Drizzle with the remaining cream and garnish with coriander leaves.

5 Try serving this with mushroom rice (p157) and bhindi masala (p165).

Per serving of curry without rice and side dish: 1840kJ/439kcal (22%), 21.8g fat (31%), 12.7g saturates (64%), 12.9g sugars (14%), 0.78g salt (13%)

66

Meat

meat

Keema curry

This delicious beef curry is easy to make and mild enough for all the family to enjoy. If you want to turn up the heat, use hot curry powder

1 tbsp vegetable oil
1 onion, finely chopped
1 clove garlic, finely chopped
2.5cm piece fresh ginger, peeled and finely chopped
500g pack extra-lean beef steak mince by Sainsbury's
1 tbsp mild curry powder

2 tbsp tomato purée
500ml beef stock made with 1 stock cube
390g carton chopped tomatoes by Sainsbury's
1 tbsp tomato ketchup
50g frozen peas
5 spring onions, trimmed and chopped, to garnish

1 Heat the oil in a large deep frying pan over a medium heat. Add the onion, garlic and ginger, and fry for 5-6 mins, until softened.

2 Add the mince and stir-fry for 6-7 mins, stirring occasionally, until brown all over. Stir in the curry powder and cook for a further min. Add the tomato purée, beef stock, chopped tomatoes and ketchup, and mix well. Simmer for 15 mins, until the liquid has reduced and thickened. About 3 mins before the end of the cooking time, add the peas to the curry. Garnish with chopped spring onions to serve.

3 We suggest serving this curry with jeera rice (p156).

Per serving of curry without rice: 1041kJ/248kcal (12%), 9.2g fat (13%), 2.9g saturates (15%), 7.7g sugars (9%), 1.12g salt (19%)

Cook's tip
Make this vegetarian by replacing the beef mince with meat-free mince by Sainsbury's and using a vegetable stock cube.

HEAT
SERVES 4
PREP TIME 10
mins, plus 30 mins
marinating
COOK TIME
about 45 mins

Lamb balti

Balti refers to the metal bowl first used in Indian restaurants in the West Midlands to deliver fast and fresh tomato-based curries like this one

411g pack diced lamb by Sainsbury's
Zest and juice of 1 lime
1 tbsp vegetable oil
1 onion, chopped
2cm piece fresh ginger, peeled and chopped
1 clove garlic, crushed
2 tbsp balti paste (p9) or 4 tbsp
balti paste by Sainsbury's

390g carton chopped tomatoes
by Sainsbury's
1 tsp sugar
1 red pepper, deseeded and roughly chopped
200g bag sugar snaps by Sainsbury's
Small handful chopped fresh coriander,
to garnish

1   Put the lamb in a non-metallic dish and stir in the lime zest and juice. Cover and leave to marinate in a cool place for 30 mins.

2   Heat the oil in a large deep frying pan over a medium heat. Add the onion and fry for 5 mins, until softened. Add the ginger and garlic, and cook for 1 min, then stir in the balti paste, lower the heat and cook, stirring, for a further min.

3   Add the lamb to the pan and stir-fry over a medium-high heat for 5-6 mins, until no longer pink. Add the tomatoes, sugar, red pepper and 100ml water, and bring to the boil. Reduce the heat, cover and simmer for 20 mins, stirring occasionally.

4   Meanwhile, blanch the sugar snaps in a pan of boiling water for 1 min. Drain and refresh under cold water. Set aside.

5   Add the sugar snaps to the pan and simmer, uncovered, for 5-10 mins, stirring occasionally, until the lamb is tender. Season to taste and garnish with coriander. This dish goes really well with onion parathas (p159).

Per serving of curry without parathas: 1644kJ/399kcal (20%), 23g fat (33%), 9.5g saturates (48%), 11g sugars (12%), 0.01g salt (0%)

Cook's tip
Make this a prawn balti by marinating 2 x 180g packs raw king prawns by Sainsbury's as described in step 1, then add to the pan with the sugar snaps in step 5.

HEAT
SERVES 4
PREP TIME
20-25 mins
COOK TIME
30 mins, plus resting
2 of 5 A-DAY

Sri Lankan pork curry

Although Sri Lankan cuisine shares some similarities to the food of south India, the spicing is subtly different – but just as delicious!

2 tsp medium curry powder

500g pork tenderloin fillet (from the meat counter)

3 tbsp vegetable oil

Few fresh curry leaves, washed

1 lemon grass stalk, bruised and finely chopped

4 cardamom pods, lightly crushed

1 cinnamon stick

3 whole cloves

1 onion, roughly chopped

300g pack dwarf beans by Sainsbury's, trimmed

175g pack okra by Sainsbury's

3 cloves garlic, finely chopped

4cm piece fresh ginger, peeled and finely chopped

1 tsp hot chilli powder

1 tbsp rice vinegar

1 tsp tamarind paste by Sainsbury's

400ml tin reduced-fat coconut milk

250g cooked basmati rice, to serve

1   Preheat the oven to 180°C, fan 160°C, gas 4. Rub half the curry powder into the pork. Heat half the oil in a frying pan over a medium heat and cook the pork for 3-4 mins, until just golden on all sides. Transfer to a roasting tin and roast for 20-25 mins until golden and cooked through. Remove from the oven and rest for 10 mins.

2   Meanwhile, heat the remaining oil and add the curry leaves, lemon grass, cardamom pods, cinnamon stick and cloves. Fry for 2-3 mins, until fragrant, then add the onion, beans and okra, and continue to fry for 3-4 mins. Stir in the garlic, ginger, chilli powder and remaining curry powder, and cook for 1 min. Stir in the vinegar, tamarind paste, coconut milk and 300ml water. Bring to a gentle simmer and cook for 10 mins, then remove the cinnamon stick.

3   Slice the pork, season with freshly ground black pepper and serve with the vegetable curry and cooked basmati rice.

Per serving of curry with rice: 2484kJ/591kcal (30%), 21.2g fat (30%), 8.6g saturates (43%), 6.9g sugars (8%), 0.27g salt (5%)

Cook's tip
Also called lady's fingers or bhindi, okra goes well with garlic, ginger and chilli. Try using it in stir-fries.

Lamb curry with butternut squash

Lamb loves butternut squash, especially when they are cooked together in a gently warming curry sauce and served with basmati rice

Sunflower oil spray
1 onion, sliced
325g lamb leg steaks (from the meat counter), cut into chunks
1 medium butternut squash, peeled, deseeded and cubed
6 tbsp Thai red curry paste (p10) or
½ jar Thai red curry paste by Sainsbury's

400ml tin reduced fat coconut milk
400ml chicken or vegetable stock made with 1 stock cube
150g low-fat natural yogurt
Large handful fresh basil, leaves shredded
Large handful fresh coriander, chopped
Zest and juice of 1 lime
250g basmati rice, cooked, to serve

1   Add a spray of oil to a large non-stick pan, add the onion and cook over a medium heat for 8-10 mins, until softened. Transfer to a plate.

2   Add the lamb to the pan in batches to brown. Transfer each batch to the plate with the onion as you cook.

3   Return the onion and lamb to the pan and add the butternut squash cubes. Stir and cover. Cook for 5 mins, then remove the lid and cook for a further 5 mins or until the excess juices have evaporated.

4   Stir in the curry paste and cook, stirring, for a further 30 seconds, then pour in the coconut milk and stock. Season to taste, then bring to the boil. Reduce the heat and simmer the curry, uncovered, for 30 mins or until the meat is tender and the squash is cooked through.

5   Stir in the yogurt, basil, coriander and lime zest and juice, and heat through. Serve with the cooked basmati rice.

Per serving of curry with rice: 2577kJ/613kcal (31%), 22.3g fat (32%), 11.9g saturates (60%), 12.7g sugars (14%), 1.25g salt (21%)

Sainsbury's
magazine
RECIPE

HEAT
SERVES 4
PREP TIME
10-15 mins
COOK TIME
1 hour 25 mins

Cambodian pork & coconut curry

Cambodian food features fresh ingredients and a more restrained use of spices. You'll notice the subtle differences in this fragrant pork curry

2 tbsp vegetable oil

420g pack British pork shoulder steaks by Sainsbury's, diced

1 aubergine, trimmed and diced

180g jar laksa paste by Sainsbury's

1 tsp turmeric

500g butternut squash, peeled, deseeded and diced

400ml tin reduced fat coconut milk

1½ tbsp fish sauce

1 tsp palm sugar by Sainsbury's

1 tsp tamarind paste by Sainsbury's

Juice of 1 lime, plus extra lime wedges to serve

Handful fresh basil leaves

Few fresh coconut pieces by Sainsbury's, grated, to garnish

250g basmati rice, cooked, to serve

1   Heat half the oil in a large pan. Add the pork and fry for 2-3 mins, until browned all over. You may need to do this in batches. Remove from the pan and set aside.

2   Heat the remaining oil in the same pan, add the aubergine and cook for 4-5 mins, until golden. Return the pork to the pan with the laksa paste and turmeric. Cook for 1-2 mins, until the paste has become fragrant, then add the diced squash, the coconut milk and 300ml water. Gently bring to the boil, then reduce the heat to a simmer and cook, covered, for 1 hour, or until the pork is tender.

3   Stir in the fish sauce, palm sugar, tamarind paste, lime juice and half the basil leaves, and simmer gently, uncovered, for 10 mins. Season to taste, then serve garnished with the fresh grated coconut, remaining basil leaves and extra lime wedges, with cooked rice on the side.

Per serving of curry with rice: 2648kJ/631kcal (32%), 25.7g fat (37%), 12.2g saturates (61%), 15.3g sugars (17%), 3g salt (50%)

Cook's tip
Instead of butternut squash, try adding halved new potatoes or roughly chopped carrots.

Lamb biryani

Try this all-in-one lamb curry and rice dish – it's a winner!

2 onions, 1 finely chopped and 1 thinly sliced

2 cloves garlic, crushed

3cm piece fresh ginger, peeled and grated

¼ tsp saffron strands

3 tbsp milk, warmed

5 tbsp vegetable oil

2 x 300g packs diced lamb by Sainsbury's

1-2 tbsp madras paste (p9) or 3 tbsp madras paste by Sainsbury's

275g low-fat natural yogurt

350g basmati rice

15g butter

1 tbsp flaked almonds

Fresh coriander leaves, to garnish

1   Put the chopped onion, garlic and ginger in a food processor with 2 tbsp water. Process to a paste, then set aside. Soak the saffron in the milk in a small bowl.

2   Meanwhile, heat 2 tbsp oil in a large frying pan over a medium-high heat, add the lamb and cook for 3 mins, until browned – you may need to do this in batches. Remove from the pan and set aside. Reduce the heat to medium, add 1 tbsp of the remaining oil and the onion paste, and fry for 3-4 mins, stirring, until golden. Stir in the madras paste and cook for 1-2 mins. Return the lamb to the pan and gradually add the yogurt. Season to taste, cover and simmer gently for 40 mins, stirring occasionally, until the lamb is tender. Spoon into a large casserole.

3   Meanwhile, bring a large pan of water to the boil, add the rice and cook for 10 mins. Drain well.

4   Preheat the oven to 160°C, fan 140°C, gas 3. Pile the cooked rice on top of the lamb mixture to cover completely and form a mound. Make a hole in the centre of the rice mound. Dot the rice with the butter, then drizzle over the saffron-infused milk. Cover tightly and bake for 1 hour, or until the rice is tender.

5   About 15 mins before the end of the cooking time, heat the rest of the oil in a frying pan and fry the almonds until golden. Drain on kitchen paper. Add the sliced onion to the pan and fry until crisp and golden. Drain on kitchen paper.

6   To serve, fluff up the rice with a fork and spoon it out onto a warmed platter, then pile the lamb on top. Scatter over the almonds, onions and coriander leaves. This biryani goes really well with our spiced carrot & radish salad (p165).

Per serving without salad: 4171kJ/996kcal (50%), 49.2g fat (70%), 17.5g saturates (88%), 11g sugars (12%), 0.1g salt (2%)

HEAT
SERVES 4
PREP TIME 15 mins
COOK TIME
2 hours 15 mins

Vietnamese beef curry

This aromatic curry is slow-cooked, which makes the beef
meltingly tender. Serve it with noodles for a change from rice

3 tbsp vegetable oil

600g braising steak (from the meat
counter), cubed

600ml beef stock, made with 1 stock cube

2 lemon grass stalks, bruised, outer leaves
removed and finely chopped

2 cloves garlic, finely chopped

5cm piece fresh ginger, peeled and
finely chopped

3 whole star anise

2 red chillies, sliced

2 tsp medium curry powder

1 cinnamon stick

1½ tsp Chinese five spice

3 tbsp tomato purée

3 large carrots, peeled and cut into
large chunks

2 x 300g packs rice noodles by Sainsbury's

Lime wedges, to serve

1   Heat half the oil in a large pan over a medium heat and brown the beef for
    3-4 mins, then remove and set aside. You may need to do this in batches. Pour
    100ml of the stock into the pan and bring to the boil. Boil for 1 min to deglaze
    the pan, loosening the bits stuck to the bottom with a spatula, then transfer to
    a heatproof jug and set aside.

2   Heat the remaining oil in the pan and fry the lemon grass, garlic and ginger for
    1 min. Stir in the star anise, red chillies, curry powder, cinnamon stick and Chinese
    five spice. Cook for a further min, until fragrant, then stir the beef back into the
    pan with the tomato purée, carrots, remaining stock and the deglazing stock in
    the jug. Reduce the heat, cover, and simmer gently for 2 hours, until the beef is
    tender. Season to taste with freshly ground black pepper.

3   Put the noodles in a heatproof bowl, pour over boiling water and let soak for 3
    mins. Drain well, then serve with the curry and the lime wedges to squeeze over.

Per serving with rice noodles: 3148kJ/752kcal (38%), 37.2g fat (53%), 12.9g
saturates (65%), 9.5g sugars (11%), 1.5g salt (25%)

Drink suggestion
Try a crisp white wine, such as Taste the Difference
Awatere Valley Riesling, with this dish.

HEAT
SERVES 4
PREP TIME
15-20 mins
COOK TIME
2 hours 20 mins

Beef madras

Madras curries are renowned for their heat, rich colour and full flavour

2 tbsp vegetable oil

2 onions, sliced

500g braising steak (from the meat counter), cut into chunks

3 tbsp madras paste (p9), or

6 tbsp madras paste by Sainsbury's

2 tbsp tomato purée

390g carton chopped tomatoes by Sainsburys

400ml beef stock, made with 1 stock cube by Sainsbury's

260g pack young spinach by Sainsbury's

4 tbsp single cream

Handful fresh coriander, roughly chopped

1 Heat the oil in a large pan and fry the onions for 5-10 mins, until softened and golden. Add the beef and stir-fry for 2-3 mins, until it starts to brown, then add the madras paste. Cook for 2-3 mins, until fragrant.

2 Stir in the tomato purée, chopped tomatoes and stock, and bring to the boil. Turn the heat down and simmer, covered, for 2 hours, until the beef is tender and the sauce has thickened, stirring occasionally. Stir in the spinach and cook for a further min, until just wilted, then season to taste with black pepper.

3 Serve in bowls, drizzled with the cream and sprinkled with chopped coriander. This is a great dish to have with chapattis (p159).

Per serving of curry without chapattis: 2155kJ/517kcal (26%), 31.4g fat (45%), 12.4g saturates (62%), 9.2g sugars (10%), 1.41g salt (24%)

meat

Beef rendang

A colourful Malaysian-style curry with a sprinkling of toasted coconut

2 tbsp vegetable oil

2 cinnamon sticks

457g pack lean casserole steak by Sainsbury's

4-5 tbsp rendang paste (p10), or 190g jar rendang paste by Sainsbury's

1 red chilli, sliced

400ml tin reduced fat coconut milk

1 tbsp dark brown soft sugar

2 tsp tamarind paste by Sainsbury's

1 red and 1 orange pepper, deseeded and sliced

25g desiccated coconut, toasted (see cook's tip)

Juice of 1 lime

Small handful fresh coriander, roughly chopped

1 Heat the oil in a large pan and add the cinnamon. Fry for 1 min, then add the beef and cook for about 5 mins, until brown on all sides - you may need to do this in batches. Return all the beef to the pan, then add the rendang paste and chilli. Cook for 2-3 mins, until the spices become fragrant and the paste has begun to darken. Gradually add the coconut milk, sugar, and tamarind, and season to taste.

2 Bring to a gentle simmer and cook for about 2 hours, until the beef is tender and the sauce has reduced and thickened. Towards the end of the cooking time, you will need to keep stirring the rendang to stop it from catching on the bottom of the pan.

3 Add the peppers and half the toasted coconut to the rendang halfway into the cooking time. Once the sauce has reach your desired thickness, cover with a lid so no more of the liquid evaporates. If it has become too thick, add a little water.

4 Add the lime juice and garnish with the remaining toasted coconut and chopped coriander. This goes really well with sticky rice (p40).

Per serving of curry without rice: 1494kJ/358kcal (18%), 20.9g fat (30%), 12.1g saturates (61%), 13.5g sugars (15%), 0.34g salt (6%)

Cook's tip
To toast the coconut, put in a pan and cook over a medium heat, stirring until it begins to turn brown. Tip out of the pan once you have the colour you want.

HEAT
SERVES 4
PREP TIME
15-20 mins,
plus at least
2 hours marinating
COOK TIME 30 mins

Lamb pasanda

This version of the classic curry uses a butterflied leg of lamb, rather than diced meat. Try serving with pilau rice (p157) and bhindi masala (p165)

2 green chillies, chopped

1 tbsp garam masala

65g cashew nuts, chopped

400g be good to yourself Greek-style natural yogurt

1 tsp ground cumin

1 tsp ground coriander

1 butterflied lamb leg, about 650g

2 tbsp vegetable oil

1 onion, finely chopped

6 cardamom pods, gently crushed, pods discarded and seeds crushed

1 cinnamon stick

3 cloves garlic, finely chopped

4cm piece fresh ginger, peeled and finely chopped

4 tbsp half-fat crème fraîche

1   Put the chillies, garam masala, cashews and 4 tbsp of the yogurt in a food processor and blend to a smooth paste. Transfer to a bowl and stir in the remaining yogurt, then add the cumin and coriander.

2   Pierce the leg of lamb several times, making sure some of the slits go all the way through the meat. Put the lamb in a large roasting dish and pour over the yogurt marinade. Massage it into the lamb, pushing it all the way into the slits. Cover with cling film and leave to marinate in the fridge for 2 hours or overnight.

3   Bring the lamb to room temperature. Preheat the oven to 190°C, fan 170°C, gas 5. Remove the lamb from the marinade, scraping most of it off. Heat half the oil in a large pan and fry the lamb on each side for 4-5 mins, until golden, then transfer to a shallow roasting tin and cook in the oven for 25-30 mins (for medium) or 40-45 mins (for well done). Remove from the oven and rest for 10 mins.

4   Meanwhile, heat the remaining oil in a large pan and cook the onion, cardamom seeds and cinnamon stick for 5-10 mins, until softened, adding the garlic and ginger for the last 2 mins. Pour in the marinade from the lamb and bring to a gentle simmer. Remove from the heat and stir through the crème fraîche, then serve alongside slices of the lamb. This goes really well with pilau rice (p157) and bhindi masala (p165).

Per serving of curry without rice and side dish: 2692kJ/647kcal (32%), 45.9g fat (66%), 18.7g saturates (94%), 10.7g sugars (12%), 1.07g salt (18%)

HEAT
SERVES 4
PREP TIME 25-30 mins, plus chilling
COOK TIME 2 hours 40 mins

Thai beef massaman

A popular Thai curry that has a hint of sweetness. Serve it with basmati and wild rice, for something a little different

2 tbsp vegetable oil
457g pack lean diced casserole beef steak, by Sainsburys
500ml beef stock, made with 1 stock cube
1 onion, finely sliced
3-4 tbsp massaman paste (p10), or 190g jar massaman curry paste by Sainsbury's
3 bay leaves

500g baby potatoes, halved
75g raw unsalted peanuts
1 red chilli, sliced
400ml tin reduced-fat coconut milk
1 tbsp light brown soft sugar
1 tbsp fish sauce
250g basmati & wild rice by Sainsbury's, cooked, to serve

1   Heat the oil in a large pan and brown the beef on all sides for 3-4 mins. You may need to do this in batches. Remove the meat from the pan and set aside.

2   Add 100ml of the stock to the pan and bring to the boil over a medium-high heat, scraping up any bits of meat stuck to the bottom of the pan. Turn the heat down to low and add the onion. Cook for 5-10 mins, until softened, then return the beef to the pan and add the massaman paste. Stir together for 2-3 mins. Stir in the remaining stock, bay leaves, potatoes, 50g of the peanuts and half the chilli, then gradually stir in the coconut milk.

3   Bring to a gentle simmer, then cover and cook for 1 hour 30 mins. Remove the lid and continue to cook over a very gentle heat for another 30-45 mins, until the meat is tender and the sauce is slightly thickened.

4   Stir the sugar and fish sauce into the curry. Ladle into bowls and top with the remaining peanuts and chilli. Serve with the cooked rice.

Per serving of curry with rice: 2966kJ/706kcal (35%), 25.3g fat (36%), 9.4g saturates (47%), 12g sugars (13%), 2.3g salt (38%)

Goan hot & sour pork

HEAT
SERVES 4
PREP TIME
20 mins, plus at
least 2-3 hours
marinating
COOK TIME
1 hour 30 mins

Tamarind and vinegar give this delicious curry a bit of a
tang, while the ginger and coriander keep the flavours fresh

420g pack pork shoulder steaks
by Sainsbury's, diced
4 tbsp Goan masala paste (p9),
or ½ x 300g jar Goan masala paste
2 tbsp vegetable oil
1 onion, finely chopped
2 garlic cloves, finely chopped
2cm piece fresh ginger, peeled and
finely grated

1 tsp turmeric
3 tbsp cider vinegar by Sainsbury's
1 tsp mustard seeds
½ tbsp tamarind paste by Sainsbury's
1 red chilli, sliced, to garnish
2 tbsp chopped fresh coriander, to garnish

1   Put the pork in a large bowl with half the paste. Stir to coat, then cover and
     set aside to marinate in the fridge for 2-3 hours, or longer if you have time.

2   Heat half the oil in a large pan over a medium heat and cook the onion for
     10 mins, until softened and turning golden. Transfer to a food processor and
     whizz together with the garlic, ginger, turmeric, vinegar and 2 tbsp water, until
     blended and smooth.

3   In the same pan, heat the remaining oil, add the mustard seeds and fry for
     1 min, until beginning to pop. Stir in the onion mixture and the remaining Goan
     masala paste, and fry for 1-2 mins until fragrant. Stir in the pork and fry for a
     further 5 mins. Add 250ml water, bring to a simmer and cook, covered, over
     a low heat for 1 hour, or until the pork is tender. Stir the tamarind paste into the
     pan and continue to cook for 10 mins before serving, garnished with sliced chilli
     and chopped coriander.

4   If you like, serve with spicy basmati rice with coriander & mint (p157) and
     cabbage poriyal (p162).

Per serving without rice and side dish: 1157kJ/278kcal (14%), 17.8g fat (25%),
5.4g saturates (27%), 5.2g sugars (6%), 0.03g salt (1%)

HEAT
SERVES 4
PREP TIME 15-20 mins, plus 2-3 hours marinating
COOK TIME
1 hour 30 mins

Lamb rogan josh

Rogan josh was originally a Persian lamb dish and is now a feature of Kashmiri cuisine. Marinating the meat keeps it nice and tender

200ml natural yogurt

2 cloves garlic, finely chopped

2cm piece fresh ginger, peeled and finely chopped

2 pinches saffron, soaked in 1 tbsp hot water

2½ tbsp vegetable oil

411g pack diced lamb by Sainsbury's

1 onion, sliced

3 tbsp rogan josh paste (p10), or 6 tbsp rogan josh paste by Sainsbury's

2 tsp garam masala

390g carton chopped tomatoes by Sainsbury's

300g pack dwarf beans by Sainsbury's, trimmed

2 tbsp chopped fresh coriander, to garnish

1 In a large bowl, mix the yogurt, garlic, ginger, saffron mixture and 1 tsp of the vegetable oil. Stir in the lamb, then cover and set aside to marinate in the fridge for 2-3 hours.

2 Heat the remaining oil in a large pan and add the onion. Cook for 5-10 mins, until turning golden, then add the rogan josh paste. Stir for 1-2 mins, then add the lamb. Bring to a gentle simmer over a low-medium heat, then add the garam masala and tomatoes. Season to taste and cook for 1 hour 15 mins, or until the lamb is tender. Stir in the beans 15 mins before the end of the cooking time. Garnish with coriander to serve.

3 Try this curry with (uncoloured) pilau rice (p157) and a side of Bombay potatoes (p164), if you like.

Per serving of curry without rice and side dish: 1952kJ/468kcal (23%), 29.4g fat (42%), 10.3g saturates (52%), 10.5g sugars (12%), 0.11g salt (2%)

Drink suggestion
A full-flavoured red wine, such as Winemakers' Selection South Australia Shiraz will go especially well with this curry.

HEAT
SERVES 4
PREP TIME 20 mins, plus 2-3 hours marinating and 8-10 hours soaking time
COOK TIME 3 hours 25 mins

Dhal gosht with lamb

A hearty all-in-one dish of lamb, tomatoes and split peas

175g yellow split peas by Sainsbury's
4 cloves garlic, finely chopped
3cm piece fresh ginger, peeled and finely chopped
2 tsp ground cumin
2 tsp ground coriander
2 tsp chilli powder
4 tsp garam masala
380ml natural yogurt
Juice of 1 lemon

4 lamb shanks
3 tbsp vegetable oil
1 onion, sliced
1 tsp turmeric
250ml lamb stock, made with 1 stock cube by Sainsbury's
390g carton chopped tomatoes by Sainsbury's
1 tsp black mustard seeds
6 fresh curry leaves, washed

1   Put the yellow split peas in a bowl and cover with water. Cover and leave to soak for 8-10 hours, or overnight in the fridge.

2   Put half the garlic, ginger, cumin, coriander, chilli powder and garam masala in a large bowl and stir in 300ml of the yogurt and the lemon juice. Add the lamb shanks and turn the meat to coat it in the mixture. Cover and marinate in the fridge for 2-3 hours, or overnight for best results.

3   Put the split peas in a pan. Cover with fresh water, bring to the boil and cook for 10 mins. Drain.

4   Preheat the oven to 150°C, fan 130°C, gas 2. Heat 2 tbsp vegetable oil in a large casserole and cook the onion for 5-10 mins, adding the remaining garlic and ginger for the last 1-2 mins of the cooking time. Add the turmeric and the remaining spices, followed by the lamb with the marinade, then the stock, tomatoes and split peas. Season to taste, bring to a simmer, cover and cook in the oven for 2½-3 hours, until the split peas are tender and the lamb falls off the bone.

5   Towards the end of the cooking time, heat the remaining oil and fry the mustard seeds and curry leaves for 1-2 mins, until the seeds begin to pop. Ladle the curry into bowls, top with the remaining yogurt (about 1 tbsp each), the mustard seeds and curry leaves.

Per serving: 2925kJ/700kcal (35%), 37.6g fat (54%), 12.4g saturates (62%), 13g sugars (14%), 1.58g salt (26%)

Fish & seafood

Thai red fish curry

You can have this simple but delicious fish curry on the table
in just 20 mins, making it an ideal midweek family meal

1 tbsp vegetable oil

2 tbsp Thai red curry paste (p10), or 3 tbsp
red Thai paste by Sainsbury's

Small handful fresh coriander, leaves picked
and stalks finely chopped

200g pack fine beans by Sainsbury's

1 red chilli, deseeded and chopped

500ml fish stock made with 1 stock cube

1 tsp fish sauce

320g pack fish pie mix by Sainsbury's

125g young leaf spinach

400ml tin reduced-fat coconut milk

Juice of 1 lemon

1   Heat the oil in a large pan. Add the curry paste, coriander stalks, beans and
    most of the chilli, and cook over a low heat for 5 mins, then pour in the fish stock.
    Bring to a gentle simmer, then add the fish sauce. Cook for a further 5 mins.

2   Stir in the fish pie mix and cook for 2 mins. Add the spinach and coconut milk,
    then heat gently for 2-3 mins (but don't boil), until the fish is opaque and cooked
    through. Stir through the lemon juice and most of the coriander leaves.

3   Garnish with the remaining coriander and chilli. Try this curry with sticky
    rice (p40).

Per serving of curry without rice: 1011kJ/243kcal (12%), 15.8g fat (23%),
8g saturates (40%), 2.8g sugars (3%), 1.7g salt (28%)

Cook's tip
For something different, try making this recipe with
Thai green or yellow paste (p10) instead of red. The
coriander in the green paste complements the subtle
flavour of the fish, while the turmeric in the yellow
paste goes especially well with the spinach.

HEAT
SERVES 4
PREP TIME 10mins
COOK TIME 15 mins

Zanzibar fish curry

This fresh-tasting curry uses coconut milk as the base for the sauce, which marries perfectly with the sweet, delicate flavour of the sea bass

4 tbsp vegetable oil
3 echalion shallots, thicky sliced
2 cloves garlic, chopped
2cm piece fresh ginger, peeled and grated
1 red chilli, deseeded and finely sliced
2 large tomatoes, finely chopped
400ml tin reduced-fat coconut milk
1 tsp medium curry powder by Sainsbury's

1 tsp cumin seeds
1 tsp fennel seeds
2 fresh kaffir lime leaves, washed
Juice of 1 lime
1 tbsp fish sauce
2 x 180g packs boneless sea bass fillets by Sainsbury's
Handful fresh basil leaves, to garnish

1 Heat 2 tbsp of the oil in a pan, add the shallots, garlic, ginger and red chilli, and fry for 3 mins to soften.

2 Add the chopped tomatoes and coconut milk, and simmer for 5 mins.

3 Grind the curry powder with the cumin and fennel seeds using a pestle and mortar, then add to the pan with the kaffir lime leaves, lime juice and fish sauce.

4 Cut a few slashes across the skin of the sea bass fillets. Heat the remaining oil in a frying pan until hot. Add the fish, skin-side down, and fry over a high heat for 2-3 mins, until browned. Turn and cook for 2-3 mins on the other side, until the fish is cooked through.

5 Ladle the curry sauce into bowls and serve the sea bass fillets on top. Scatter over the basil leaves. You might like to serve this with boiled white rice.

Per serving of curry without rice: 1432kJ/345kcal (17%), 25.8g fat (37%), 8.6g saturates (43%), 3.8g sugars (4%), 1.08 salt (18%)

Cook's tip
If you can't get fresh kaffir lime leaves, dried ones are a good alternative, or use a grating of lime zest instead.

Prawn bhuna

Prawns, peppers, chilli and tomatoes combine to make an intensely flavoured dish. You might like to serve this with some roti (p159)

2 tbsp jalfrezi paste (p8), or 2 tbsp shop-bought jalfrezi paste

Juice of 1 lemon

2 cloves garlic, crushed

2 x 225g bags frozen Taste the Difference raw peeled jumbo king prawns, defrosted

1 tbsp groundnut oil

1 onion, chopped

1 yellow pepper, deseeded and sliced

1 green chilli, deseeded and chopped

150g cherry tomatoes

Fresh coriander leaves, to garnish

1   In a large non-metallic bowl, mix together the jalfrezi paste, lemon juice and crushed garlic. Add the prawns, stir well to coat in the spice mixture and set aside for 15 mins.

2   Meanwhile, heat the oil in a large frying pan. Add the onion, yellow pepper and half the green chilli, and cook over a medium heat for 10 mins, until soft and starting to brown.

3   Add the cherry tomatoes, cook for 2 mins, then add the prawns and their marinade. Cook for 5 mins, stirring, until the prawns are cooked through. If the mixture becomes dry, add 2-3 tbsp water to thin it slightly.

4   Sprinkle with some of the remaining sliced green chilli (put the rest in a bowl for people to help themselves to) and the coriander leaves. Serve with roti (p159), if you like.

Per serving of curry without roti: 783kJ/186kcal (9%), 6.4g fat (9%), 0.9g saturates (5%), 6.6g sugars (7%), 1.65g salt (28%)

Cook's tip
This prawn bhuna is a mild curry – if you'd prefer it to be a bit hotter, add ½-1 tsp chilli powder to the marinade with the prawns.

HEAT
SERVES 4
PREP TIME 25 mins
COOK TIME
5-10 mins

Mussels with chilli & ginger

This simple dish is quick and easy to prepare. It also makes a great starter – just halve the ingredient quantites

2kg fresh mussels (from the fish counter)
1 tbsp vegetable oil
4cm piece fresh ginger, peeled and cut into matchsticks
4 spring onions, trimmed and sliced

3 green chillies, halved, deseeded and thinly sliced
½ tsp turmeric
400ml tin reduced-fat coconut milk
4 tbsp chopped fresh coriander

1   Rinse the mussels in cold water, scrub the shells and remove any 'beards'. Discard any with shells that are damaged, or any open mussels that don't close when tapped. Set the mussels aside.

2   Heat the vegetable oil in a large pan. Add the ginger, spring onions and chillies, and fry for 1 min. Add the turmeric and coconut milk, and bring to a gentle simmer.

3   Add the mussels, cover and simmer for 4 mins, until the mussels have opened. Using a slotted spoon, transfer the mussels to bowls, discarding any that remain closed. Pour over the cooking liquid and scatter with the chopped coriander. If you like, serve with naan bread (p158) for mopping up the juices.

Per serving of curry without naan: 839kJ/201kcal (10%), 11.7g fat (17%), 7.3g saturates (37%), 3g sugars (3%), 2.56 salt (43%)

Cook's tip
For more heat, sprinkle some dried chilli flakes over the mussels with the chopped coriander before serving.

HEAT
SERVES 4
PREP TIME 10 mins
COOK TIME
20-25 mins
1 of 5 A DAY

Tandoori rainbow trout

A simple way to cook whole fish that infuses it with fragrant spices

Oil, for greasing
2 x 1.2kg packs 2 whole trout by Sainsbury's
2 limes, thinly sliced
4 shallots, thinly sliced
1-2 tbsp tandoori paste (p9) or 1-2 tbsp shop-bought tandoori paste

¼ tsp sea salt flakes (optional)
200g green salad leaves
200g cherry tomatoes, halved
Lime wedges, shredded spring onions and fresh mint leaves, to garnish

1 Preheat the oven to 200ºC, fan 180ºC, gas 6. Grease a large non-stick roasting tin with the oil. Use a sharp knife to cut 4 slashes in the flesh of one side of each trout. Arrange the fish, slashed-side up, in the roasting tin. Push the sliced limes and shallots into the cavity of each fish.

2 Spread the tandoori paste in a thin layer over the fish, rubbing it into the slashed flesh. Sprinkle over the sea salt, if using.

3 Roast for 20-22 mins, until the skin is crisp and the fish is cooked through and flakes easily. Serve with the green salad leaves tossed with the cherry tomatoes. Garnish the fish with the lime wedges, shredded spring onion and fresh mint leaves. Try serving this with pilau rice (p157) and lime pickle (p160).

Per serving without rice and pickle: 2293kJ/548kcal (27%), 27.2g fat (39%), 5.1g saturates (26%), 3.9g sugars (4%), 0.54g salt (9%)

Ginger & cardamom tea

Put 50g peeled and grated fresh ginger in a pan with 6 lightly crushed cardamom pods and 1 litre water. Bring to the boil, then simmer for 3 mins. Add 2 Darjeeling tea bags, remove from the heat, cover and leave to infuse for 2-3 mins. Strain into glasses, add a thin slice of lemon to each glass and serve.

Serves 4 Prep time: 10 mins Cook time: 5 mins (plus infusing)
Per serving: 67kJ/16kcal (1%), <1g fat (<0.5%), <0.1g saturates (<1%), 0.8g sugars (1%), <0.01g salt (<1%)

HEAT
SERVES 4
PREP TIME 10 mins
COOK TIME 25 mins

Sri Lankan fish curry

This colourful dish of sea bass, fresh tomatoes and green beans looks so appetising - serve it with pilau rice (p157) for a satisfying meal

2 tbsp groundnut oil

2 onions, finely sliced

1 tsp mustard seeds

1 tsp cumin seeds

1 tsp fennel seeds

2cm piece fresh ginger, peeled and chopped

2 cloves garlic, crushed

2 red chillies, deseeded and chopped

10 fresh curry leaves, washed

2 tsp ground turmeric

1 tbsp medium curry powder by Sainsbury's

200ml fish stock made with 1 stock cube

200ml coconut milk

2 x 180g packs boneless sea bass fillets by Sainsbury's, skin removed

4 tomatoes, roughly chopped

200g pack fine beans by Sainsbury's, halved

1 Heat the oil in a pan, add the onions and fry for 10 mins over a medium heat until very soft and just starting to colour.

2 Lightly crush the mustard seeds, cumin seeds and fennel seeds with a pestle and mortar, or in a small bowl with the end of rolling pin. Add to the pan with the ginger, garlic, chillies, curry leaves, turmeric and curry powder, and cook over a low heat for 2-3 mins.

3 Pour in the stock and coconut milk, bring to the boil, then reduce the heat. Add the sea bass fillets and tomatoes, and simmer, covered, for 8-10 mins, depending on the thickness of the fish, until the fish is opaque, cooked through and flakes easily.

4 Meanwhile, blanch the green beans in boiling water for 3-5 mins. Stir the beans through the curry and gently flake the fish into chunks just before serving. Serve with pilau rice (p157), if you like.

Per serving of curry without rice: 1522kJ/365kcal (18%), 22.8g fat (33%), 9.9g saturates (50%), 9.7g sugars (11%), 1.14g salt (19%)

Cook's tip
For a delicious dessert, use the leftover coconut milk from this recipe to drizzle over the fruit chaat on p168.

Malaysian fish curry

With lots of heat from the chilli heat and strong flavours, this hot fish curry makes a satisfying meal. Try serving it with homemade roti

1 large onion, roughly chopped

5cm piece fresh ginger, peeled and roughly chopped

2 cloves garlic, peeled

1 lemon grass stalk, outer leaves removed, roughly chopped

1 tsp hot chilli powder

1 tsp shrimp paste

1 tbsp madras paste (p9), or 2 tbsp madras paste by Sainsbury's

200ml reduced-fat coconut milk

½ tbsp vegetable oil

250g butternut squash, peeled and cut into cubes

3 large tomatoes, each cut into 8 slim wedges

500g skinless halibut fillet or cod loin (from the fish counter), cut into medium chunks

1 pak choi, trimmed and leaves separated

Juice of 1 lime

1   Put the onion, ginger, garlic and lemon grass in a food processor and process until finely chopped.

2   Add the chilli powder, shrimp paste and curry paste, and process again. Add 1 tbsp of the coconut milk and blend to make a paste.

3   Heat the oil in a deep frying pan, add the paste and cook for 3-4 mins, stirring frequently until fragrant. Stir in the remaining coconut milk and bring to the boil, stirring. Add the butternut squash and tomatoes. Cover and simmer for 10 mins until the squash is tender.

4   Add the fish and pak choi to the pan, then simmer gently for a further 5-8 mins, until the fish is cooked through and flakes easily. Squeeze over the lime juice to serve. Try this dish with some roti, if you like (p159).

Per serving of curry without roti: 993kJ/236kcal (12%), 5.9g fat (8%), 3.7g saturates (19%), 7.7g sugars (9%), 0.67g salt (10%)

Drink suggestion
This curry will go well with a Spanish red, such as Winemakers' Selection Gran Reserva Cariñena.

HEAT
SERVES 4
PREP TIME 10 mins
COOK TIME 25 mins

Keralan fish curry

Curries from the southern Indian state of Kerala often feature coconut milk and fish – the region is known for its wide range of seafood

240g pack 2 boneless Scottish salmon fillets by Sainsbury's, skin removed and cut into chunks

260g pack cod fillets by Sainsbury's, cut into chunks

2 tsp ground turmeric

½ tsp salt

2 tbsp groundnut oil

2 onions, sliced

1 red chilli, deseeded and sliced

2 tsp hot chilli powder

2 tbsp jalfrezi paste (p8), or 2 tbsp shop-bought jalfrezi paste

1 tsp ground cumin

1 tbsp tamarind paste

400ml tin reduced-fat coconut milk

Small handful fresh coriander, roughly chopped

Lime wedges, to serve

1   Put the salmon and white fish in a non-metallic bowl. Sprinkle over 1 tsp of the turmeric and the salt, and turn to coat. Set aside.

2   Heat the oil in a pan, add the onions and cook over a medium heat for 10 mins, until very soft and just starting to brown.

3   Add the red chilli and fry for 2 mins. Mix together the remaining turmeric and chilli powder with a splash of hot water, then stir into the pan with the jalfrezi paste, cumin and tamarind paste, and cook for a further 2 mins.

4   Stir in the coconut milk and the fish chunks, bring to the boil and simmer for 5-8 mins, until the fish is cooked through and flakes easily. Stir through most of the chopped coriander. Serve the curry with lime wedges to squeeze over, garnished with the remaining coriander. We suggest serving this with (uncoloured) pilau rice (p157).

Per serving of curry without rice: 1518kJ/364kcal (18%), 20.9g fat (30%), 9.2g saturates (46%), 8g sugars (9%), 0.67g salt (11%)

Cook's tip
Tamarind paste gives a slightly sour, fresh-tasting, flavour to curries. If you don't have any, a squeeze of lime juice at the end of the cooking time is a good alternative.

Goan fish curry

Pineapple and tamarind give this dish a delicious sweet-and-sour flavour. For something different, serve it with poppadoms, instead of rice

1 ½ tbsp vegetable oil

½ tsp mustard seeds

4 fresh curry leaves, washed

2 onions, chopped

Juice of 1 lime

½ tsp turmeric

2 x 300g packs basics pollock fillets, cut into chunks

4 tbsp Goan masala paste (p9) or

150g Goan masala paste by Sainsbury's

1 whole star anise

1 tsp tamarind paste by Sainsbury's

1 green finger chilli by Sainsbury's

3 tomatoes, chopped

500ml fish stock made with 1 stock cube

200g fresh pineapple, peeled, cored and chopped

1   Heat ½ tbsp of the oil in a large frying pan, add the mustard seeds and curry leaves and fry over a medium heat for 1-2 mins, until the mustard seeds begin to pop. Remove from the pan and set aside. Add the remaining oil to the pan and fry the onions for 10 mins, until very soft and just starting to colour.

2   Meanwhile, mix together the lime juice and turmeric in a large non-metallic bowl. Add the fish, turn to coat in the marinade, season to taste and set aside for 5 mins.

3   Add the curry paste to the onions, fry for 1 min, then add the star anise, tamarind paste, whole chilli and the chopped tomatoes. Pour in the fish stock, bring to the boil, then reduce the heat, cover and simmer for 10-15 mins, until thickened.

4   Add the fish with its marinade and the pineapple, and gently poach for 5 mins, until the fish is cooked through and flakes easily. Garnish with fried mustard seeds and curry leaves. Serve with poppadoms, if you like.

Per serving without poppadoms: 1078kJ/256kcal (13%), 7g fat (10%), 1.2g saturates (6%), 13.5g sugars (15%), 0.86g salt (14%)

Cook's tip
Pollock is an inexpensive fish that's ideal for using in a curry. Its slightly off-white colour is disguised by the colour of the spices.

HEAT 🌶🌶
SERVES 4
PREP TIME 30 mins
COOK TIME 20 mins

Fish laksa

A Malaysian-style dish of noodles, fish and veg in a coconut-based soup

260g pack cod fillets by Sainsbury's,
cut into chunks
1 tsp toasted sesame oil by Sainsbury's
1 tbsp groundnut oil
1 lemon grass stalk, outer leaves
removed, sliced
180g jar laksa paste by Sainsbury's
400ml tin reduced-fat coconut milk
300ml fish stock made with 1 stock cube
2 tsp fish sauce

Juice of 1 lime
2 tsp sambal oelek
½ x 225g bag Taste the Difference frozen
raw peeled jumbo king prawns, defrosted
100g beansprouts
300g bag fresh rice noodles by Sainsbury's
25g unsalted peanuts, chopped
50g piece cucumber, cut into thin sticks
Shredded fresh mint leaves and thinly sliced
red chilli, to garnish

1   Process the fish in a food processor until finely chopped. Gradually blend in
    4 tbsp cold water until it forms a thick purée. Using a teaspoon, shape the
    mixture into 20 balls. As you make the balls drop them into a bowl of cold water.

2   Heat the sesame oil and groundnut oil in a pan. Add the lemon grass and laksa
    paste, heat for 1 min, then pour in the coconut milk and fish stock. Gradually
    bring to the boil, then reduce the heat and simmer for 5 mins.

3   Stir in the fish sauce, lime juice and sambal oelek. Remove the fish balls from
    the bowl of water using a slotted spoon and drop them into the laksa pan
    with the prawns. Poach for 8-10 mins, until the fish balls are just firm and the
    prawns are cooked through. Add the beansprouts and rice noodles for the final
    2 mins of the cooking time.

4   Divide the laksa between 4 bowls. Scatter the peanuts and cucumber over the
    top and garnish with mint leaves and red chilli.

Per serving: 1679kJ/401cal (20%), 19.1g fat (27%), 8.5g saturates (43%),
7.9g sugars (9%), 3.85g salt (64%)

Drink suggestion
Try serving this with an ice-cold beer, such as Taste
the Difference Scottish craft brewed lager.

HEAT
SERVES 4
PREP TIME 10 mins
COOK TIME 30 mins

Smoked haddock pilau

Using smoked fish in this all-in-one dish adds another level of flavour.
Mild curry powder gives it lots of spiciness, but without too much heat

50g unsalted butter
1 onion, chopped
300g basmati rice
3 cardamom pods, lightly crushed
½ tsp turmeric
1 small cinnamon stick, broken in half
2 bay leaves
1 tbsp mild curry powder by Sainsbury's
600ml fish stock made with 1 stock cube

400g smoked haddock fillet (from the
fish counter)
100g frozen peas
2 medium eggs
3 tbsp chopped fresh flat-leaf parsley
5 spring onions, trimmed and sliced,
to garnish
Lemon wedges, to serve

1   Melt the butter in a large pan, add the onion and cook over a medium heat for
    10 mins, until soft and just starting to colour.

2   Meanwhile, rinse the rice under cold running water, until the water runs clear. Stir
    the cardamom pods, turmeric, cinnamon stick, bay leaves and curry powder into
    the pan with the onion. Cook for 2-3 mins, then add the rice and stir to coat in the
    spice mixture.

3   Pour the stock into the pan, stir well and bring to the boil. Lay the smoked
    haddock fillet on top of the rice, reduce the heat, cover and simmer for
    10 mins. Add the peas and cook for a further 5 mins, or until the fish is cooked
    through, opaque and flakes easily, and the rice is tender.

4   While the pilau is cooking, put the eggs in a pan of cold water, bring to the boil
    and simmer for 8 mins. Drain and rinse under cold water until cool enough to
    handle. Peel and cut into quarters.

5   Carefully remove the smoked haddock fillet from the pan. Remove the skin and
    break the fish into large flakes. Lightly stir the fish back into the rice with the
    parsley. Put the hard boiled egg quarters on the top, scatter over the spring
    onions and serve with the lemon wedges.

Per serving: 2294kJ/545kcal (27%), 15.4g fat (22%), 7.9g saturates (40%),
3.6g sugars (4%), 1.97g salt (33%)

HEAT
SERVES 4
PREP TIME 10 mins
COOK TIME
35-40 mins
2 of 5
A-DAY

Baked Goan monkfish

Roasting the onions and peppers first gives them a more intense, concentrated flavour in this baked fish dish

---

2 onions, cut into wedges

2 red or green peppers, deseeded and thickly sliced

2 tbsp vegetable oil

2 x 300g whole monkfish tails (from the fish counter)

5-6 tbsp Goan masala paste (p9), or 300g jar

Goan masala paste by Sainsbury's

100ml coconut milk

½ x 390g carton chopped tomatoes by Sainsbury's

1 lime, quartered, to serve

Small handful fresh coriander leaves, to garnish

---

1 Preheat the oven to 200ºC, fan 180ºC, gas 6. Put the onions and peppers on a baking tray, drizzle over the oil and toss to coat. Roast for 20 mins, until onions tender and lightly charred at the edges.

2 While the vegetables are roasting, prepare the monkfish. Cut the flesh away from either side of the central bone in each monkfish tail to make 4 fillets (you could ask for this to be done at the Sainsbury's fish counter). Season with black pepper and set aside.

3 Heat the Goan masala paste in a pan with the coconut milk and chopped tomatoes until just boiling. Pour over the roasted onions and peppers, and lay the monkfish fillets on top. Return to the oven and bake for a further 15-20 mins, until the monkfish is opaque and cooked through.

4 Serve with a squeeze of lime and a sprinkling of coriander leaves. This tastes great with a side serving of aloo gobi (p164).

Per serving of curry without aloo gobi: 1101kJ/262cal (13%), 10.5g fat (15%), 4g saturates (20%), 13.9g sugars (15%), 0.09g salt (2%)

Cook's tip
Monkfish is a firm-fleshed fish ideal for roasting and baking. You could also use halibut or chunky cod loin for this recipe.

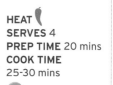

Spiced squash with prawns

Butternut squash adds a touch of sweetness to this simple but flavour-packed curry. It's delicious served with plain boiled basmati rice

1 tbsp vegetable oil
1 small onion, finely sliced
3 cloves garlic, crushed
1 green chilli, deseeded and finely chopped
¼ tsp turmeric
2 tbsp jalfrezi paste (p8) or 2 tbsp shop-bought paste by Sainsbury's
1 small butternut squash, peeled, deseeded and cubed

250ml coconut milk
2 x 225g packs frozen Taste the Difference raw jumbo king prawns, defrosted
Juice of 1 lime
Handful fresh coriander, leaves picked
Lime wedges, to serve
250g basmati rice, cooked, to serve

1   Heat the oil in a large pan and gently fry the onion, garlic and chilli for 5-7 mins, until softened. Stir in the turmeric and curry paste and fry for a further min.

2   Add the squash and coconut milk, bring to the boil, then simmer for 15 mins.

3   Stir in the prawns and lime juice, and simmer for a couple of mins until the prawns are cooked through. Season to taste. Add most of the coriander leaves and serve topped with the rest of the coriander and the remaining slices of chilli. Serve with the lime wedges and the basmati rice.

Per serving of curry with rice: 2234kJ/531cal (27%), 16.3g fat (23%), 9.2g saturates (46%), 10.1g sugars (11%), 1.65 salt (28%)

Sainsbury's
magazine
RECIPE

Vegetarian

HEAT
SERVES 4
PREP TIME 10 mins
COOK TIME 20 mins

Indian egg curry

An egg curry is a fantastic standby dish if you're after something that's filling, meat-free and quick to get on the dinner table

2 tbsp vegetable oil
1 cinnamon stick
2 cardamom pods, lightly crushed
2 shallots, finely diced
2 cloves garlic, crushed
3cm piece fresh ginger, peeled and grated
1 red chilli, deseeded and finely chopped
½ tsp hot chilli powder

1 tsp ground cumin
½ tsp ground turmeric
390g carton chopped tomatoes by Sainsbury's
300ml vegetable stock, made with 1 stock cube
Handful fresh coriander, chopped
4 large eggs

1   Heat the oil in a large deep frying pan over a medium heat, add the cinnamon stick and cardamom pods and cook for 1-2 mins, until lightly toasted and aromatic. Stir in the shallots, garlic, ginger and chilli, and cook for 3-4 mins.

2   Add the chilli powder, cumin and turmeric, and cook for 1 min, until fragrant, then pour in the chopped tomatoes and stock. Simmer for 10 mins, until the mixture has thickened, stirring occasionally. Season to taste and stir through half of the coriander.

3   Meanwhile, put the eggs in a saucepan, add cold water to cover, bring to the boil and cook over a medium heat for 8 mins. Drain the eggs and plunge into a bowl of cold water (see cook's tip). When the eggs are cool enough to handle, peel and halve them.

4   Divide the curry between 4 bowls and top each with 2 egg halves. Remove the cinnamon stick and garnish with the remaining coriander. This goes really well with chapattis (p159), if you like.

Per serving of curry without chapattis: 662kJ/159kcal (8%), 11.3g fat (16%), 2.5g saturates (13%), 3.7g sugars (4%), 1.25g salt (21%)

Cook's tip
Plunging the boiled eggs into cold water helps to prevent a grey line forming around the cooked yolks.

Sayur lodeh

A simple curried broth with tender vegetables and tofu,
this fragrantly spiced dish is popular throughout Indonesia

2 tbsp vegetable oil
5 tbsp Thai green curry paste (p10 – to make
it vegetarian replace the shrimp paste with
½ tsp dark soy sauce by Sainsbury's)
400ml tin reduced-fat coconut milk
150g green beans, trimmed

150g white cabbage, sliced
2 carrots, peeled and sliced on the diagonal
200g tofu, drained and cubed
2-3 spring onions, trimmed and sliced,
to garnish

1 Heat 1 tbsp oil in a medium saucepan and add the curry paste. Fry for 1-2 mins,
   until fragrant. Add the coconut milk and 100ml water, and bring to a simmer.

2 Add the beans, cabbage and carrots to the broth. Cover and simmer for 10 mins,
   until the vegetables are tender.

3 Meanwhile, heat the remaining vegetable oil in a frying pan over a high heat.
   Blot the tofu with kitchen paper, then fry in the hot vegetable oil. When a golden
   crust has formed on the tofu, turn and continue to fry until golden all over.
   Remove from the pan and set aside.

4 Serve the soup in bowls, topped with the fried tofu and the spring onions.

Per serving: 924kJ/222kcal (11%), 15.6g fat (22%), 7.1g saturates (36%),
8.5g sugars (9%), 0.08g salt (1%)

Cook's tip
Try to remove as much of the excess oil as possible
from the tofu before you add it to the broth.

Spinach & tofu Thai yellow curry

A lovely, delicate Thai-style curry made with young leaf spinach and tofu, which will take on all the flavours of the spices

1 tbsp vegetable oil

6 shallots, peeled and halved

396g pack tofu, drained and cubed

4 tbsp Thai yellow curry paste (p10 – to make it vegetarian replace the shrimp paste with ½ tsp dark soy sauce by Sainsbury's)

400ml tin reduced-fat coconut milk

150ml vegetable stock, made with

½ stock cube

2 fresh kaffir lime leaves, washed and finely shredded, plus extra to garnish

2 tsp palm sugar by Sainsbury's

1 tbsp soy sauce

200g bag young leaf spinach by Sainsbury's

Sliced red chilli, to garnish (optional)

1 lime, cut into wedges

1   Heat the oil in a large pan over a medium heat and fry the shallots for 8-10 mins, until softened and golden. Add the tofu and yellow curry paste, and cook, stirring, for 1 min.

2   Pour in the coconut milk and vegetable stock. Gently bring to the boil, then add the shredded lime leaves, palm sugar and fish sauce. Reduce the heat to a gentle simmer and cook for 5 mins.

3   Stir in the spinach leaves and cook for a further 2-3 mins, until just wilted. Season to taste. Serve in warmed bowls, garnished with the remaining shredded lime leaves, sliced red chilli (if using) and lime wedges to squeeze over. This is good with some sticky rice (p40), if you like.

Per serving of curry without rice: 960kJ/231kcal (12%), 14.9g fat (21%), 7.6g saturates (38%), 6.7g sugars (7%), 0.96g salt (16%)

Cook's tip
This also tastes great with noodles – try stirring a teaspoon of sesame oil into cooked egg noodles for a lovely nutty flavour.

HEAT
SERVES 4
PREP TIME
15 mins
COOK TIME
20-25 mins

Matar paneer

Paneer is a white, firm-textured Indian cheese with a mild, fresh flavour. This simple curry is one of the most popular dishes in Northern India

3 tbsp sunflower oil

227g pack paneer cheese, cut into 1.5cm cubes

2 onions, finely chopped

3 cloves garlic, crushed

1 tsp cumin seeds

5cm piece fresh ginger, peeled and finely grated

2 green chillies, deseeded and finely chopped

1 tsp ground coriander

1 tsp ground turmeric

1 tsp tomato purée

4 medium tomatoes, finely chopped

200g frozen peas

Handful fresh coriander, finely chopped

Pared lime zest, cut into thin strips, to garnish

1   Heat the oil in a large deep frying pan over a high heat for 1-2 mins. Test the temperature by dropping a piece of paneer into the oil - when it's hot enough, the oil will bubble around the cheese. Reduce the heat to medium, gently lower the paneer cubes into the oil and fry for 2-3 mins, until golden brown, turning often. Remove from the pan with a slotted spoon and drain on kitchen paper.

2   Add the onions, garlic, cumin seeds, ginger, chillies, coriander and turmeric to the hot oil and fry over a medium heat for 2-3 mins, until the onions have softened, but not browned, and the spices are aromatic.

3   Stir in the tomato purée and chopped tomatoes, then cook for 5 mins, stirring occasionally. Add the peas and 150ml water. Season to taste, reduce the heat and simmer for 2-3 mins. Return the paneer to the pan and simmer for a further 5 mins, until heated through. Garnish with the coriander and pared lime zest. This goes well with mushroom rice (p157), if you like.

Per serving of curry without rice: 1540kJ/370kcal (19%), 24.5g fat (35%), 11.2g saturates (56%), 9.6g sugars (11%), 0.07g salt (1%)

Cook's tip
Paneer will hold its shape when cooked and goes particularly well with garlic, chillies and spices. Tofu can be used in its place, but take care not to over-cook it as it will break up.

HEAT
SERVES 4
PREP TIME
10 mins
COOK TIME
25-30 mins

Sweet potato & cauliflower massaman

A mild, creamy Thai-style curry that has lots of fresh flavours

1 cauliflower, cut into small florets
2 medium sweet potatoes, peeled and diced
1 tbsp vegetable oil
3 tbsp massaman paste (p10 – to make it vegetarian replace the shrimp paste with ½ tsp dark soy sauce by Sainsbury's)
1 cinnamon stick
400ml tin reduced-fat coconut milk
300ml vegetable stock, made with

½ stock cube
2 tbsp soy sauce
Juice of ½ lime
Small handful fresh coriander, chopped, plus extra to garnish
2 tbsp dry-roasted peanuts, roughly chopped, to garnish
Red chilli, deseeded and sliced, to garnish

1   Bring a large pan of water to the boil. Add the cauliflower and sweet potato, and boil for 2-3 mins. Drain and set aside.

2   Heat the oil in a large deep pan over a high heat and add the massaman paste and cinnamon stick. Fry, stirring, for 1-2 mins, then gradually stir in the coconut milk and stock, and bring to the boil.

3   Add the cauliflower and sweet potato. Reduce the heat to a simmer and cook for 20-25 mins, until the vegetables are just tender, stirring occasionally.

4   Stir in the fish sauce, lime juice and coriander, then season to taste. Garnish with the chopped peanuts, sliced chilli and extra coriander. This is lovely served with sticky rice (p40), if you like.

Per serving of curry without rice: 1396kJ/334kcal (17%), 14.9g fat (21%), 7.5g saturates (38%), 14.9g sugars (17%), 1.66g salt (28%)

Drink suggestion
Taste the Difference Spanish Albariño is a crisp, refreshing Reisling-style white wine that goes perfectly with this vegetarian curry.

Vegetable biryani

A biryani is a rice-based dish that can be cooked with chicken, lamb (p80), fish or eggs. This is a simple vegetarian version

1 tbsp vegetable oil

1 large onion, chopped

1½ tbsp Goan masala paste (p9) or

3 tbsp Goan masala paste by Sainsbury's

½ red chilli, deseeded and finely chopped

Pinch of saffron

1 medium sweet potato, peeled and cut into 1cm cubes

1 cauliflower, cut into florets

185g basmati rice, rinsed in cold water

150g green beans, trimmed and cut into 2cm pieces

Small handful fresh coriander, chopped

1 Heat the oil in a large pan over a medium heat and fry the onion for 3-4 mins, until softened. Stir in the curry paste, chilli and saffron, and cook for 1 min. Add the sweet potato, cauliflower and rice, and stir until coated in the paste.

2 Pour over 450ml water, season to taste and stir well. Bring to the boil, then reduce the heat to a gentle simmer. Cover and cook for 15-20 mins, stirring occasionally, until the rice and vegetables are just tender and nearly all the liquid has been absorbed.

3 Stir in the beans, cover and cook for a further 3 mins. Turn off the heat and leave to stand for 2 mins, then stir through the coriander and serve.

Per serving: 1543kJ/366kcal (18%), 5.9g fat (8%), 0.9g saturates (5%), 13.2g sugars (15%), 0.12g salt (2%)

Cook's tip

You can use other vegetables for this dish – try adding peas, deseeded and diced peppers or a large handful of spinach leaves instead of the beans. For extra protein, top with 2 hard boiled eggs, quartered.

HEAT
SERVES 4
PREP TIME 15 mins
COOK TIME 30 mins

Chana masala

Chana, or chickpeas, are a staple of Indian and Pakistani cooking. Keep a couple of tins in your storecupboard to make this flavour-packed dish

1 tbsp vegetable oil
1 onion, finely chopped
4cm piece fresh root ginger, peeled and finely chopped
2 cloves garlic, finely chopped
1 green chilli, deseeded and finely chopped
2 x 410g tins chickpeas by Sainsbury's, drained and rinsed
2 tsp ground cumin

1 tbsp ground coriander
1 tsp ground turmeric
½ tsp paprika
½ tsp hot chilli powder
1 tsp garam masala
390g carton chopped tomatoes by Sainsbury's
200g bag young leaf spinach by Sainsbury's
Small handful fresh coriander, chopped

1   Heat the vegetable oil in a large deep frying pan over a medium heat and fry the onion for 5-7 mins, until softened. Add the ginger, garlic and chilli, and fry for a further 2 mins.

2   Stir in the chickpeas, cumin, coriander, turmeric, paprika, chilli powder and garam masala. Cook for 1-2 mins, until fragrant, then stir in the chopped tomatoes and 200ml water. Bring to a simmer and cook for 10-15 mins, until the sauce has thickened.

3   Stir in the spinach and season to taste. When the spinach has just wilted, stir in half the coriander. Serve in warmed bowls, garnished with the remaining coriander. Naan bread (p158) makes a great accompaniment, if you like.

Per serving without naan: 931kJ/221kcal (11%), 6.5g fat (9%), 0.8g saturates (4%), 6g sugars (7%), 0.03g salt (1%)

Cook's tip
This veggie dish tastes just as good chilled. Serve piled onto warmed naan breads with natural yogurt and mango chutney for a filling lunch or quick supper.

Aubergine & potato curry

Aubergine and potato are perfect partners in this satisfying vegetable curry – a simple yet hearty midweek supper

4 medium potatoes, peeled and cut into 2cm chunks

1 tbsp vegetable oil

2 tsp cumin seeds

2 tsp mustard seeds

Pinch of asafoetida

1 onion, finely chopped

2 aubergines, trimmed and cut into 2cm chunks

½ tsp ground turmeric

½ tsp hot chilli powder

½ tsp sugar

1 tsp ground coriander

½ tsp ground cumin

390g carton chopped tomatoes by Sainsbury's

1 tsp tamarind paste by Sainsbury's

Handful fresh coriander, chopped

1 Par-boil the potatoes in a pan of boiling water for 2-3 mins, then drain well and set aside.

2 Heat the oil in a large deep frying pan over a medium heat and add the cumin, mustard seeds and asafoetida. When the mustard seeds begin to pop (after about 1-2 mins), add the onion and aubergine chunks. Fry over a medium-high heat for 5 mins, stirring frequently, until just beginning to turn golden.

3 Stir in the turmeric, chilli powder, sugar, coriander, cumin, chopped tomatoes and 300ml water. Stir in the potatoes (making sure the liquid fully covers them) and bring to a simmer. Cover and cook for 15-20 mins, until the potatoes are tender, stirring occasionally.

4 Stir in the tamarind paste and half the fresh coriander, then cook for a further 1 min. Serve garnished with the remaining coriander.

Per serving: 1130kJ/268kcal (13%), 4.8g fat (7%), 0.3g saturates (2%), 10.6g sugars (12%), 0.07g salt (1%)

Cook's tip
For this dish, choose firm-fleshed potatoes, such as Vivaldi baking potatoes, which will hold their shape.

Rogan josh aubergines

A spicy take on a stuffed aubergine, this easy vegetarian main course can be prepared ahead of time, then finished in the oven

4 aubergines

1 tbsp olive oil

1 onion, finely chopped

3 tbsp rogan josh paste (p10) or 5 tbsp rogan josh paste by Sainsbury's

390g carton chopped tomatoes by Sainsbury's

200g bag young leaf spinach by Sainsbury's

410g tin chickpeas by Sainsbury's, drained and rinsed

4 tbsp fresh coriander, chopped

150g natural yogurt

120g mango chutney (p161)

1 Preheat the oven to 200°C, fan 180°C, gas 6. Halve the aubergines lengthways, then score the cut sides with a criss-cross pattern and place, cut-side up, in a roasting tin. Drizzle with ½ tbsp oil and roast for 30 mins, until tender.

2 Meanwhile, heat the remaining oil in a frying pan. Add the onion and cook gently, covered, for 10 mins. Stir in the rogan josh paste and cook for 2 mins. Add the tomatoes, bring to the boil, then simmer for 15 mins. Put the spinach in a large colander, pour over a kettle full of boiling water until the leaves have wilted (you may need to do this twice). Rinse under the cold tap, then squeeze out all the excess moisture and chop.

3 Scoop out the flesh from the aubergines, leaving the skins intact so you have a shell. Chop the flesh and add it to the tomato sauce. Stir in the chickpeas, spinach and half the coriander. Season to taste and cook for 5 mins.

4 Spoon the sauce into the aubergine shells and roast in the oven for 10 mins.

5 Serve topped with the yogurt and mango chutney, and garnish with the remaining coriander.

Per serving: 1226kJ/292kcal (15%), 9.3g fat (13%), 1.2g saturates (6%), 22g sugars (24%), 0.1g salt (2%)

Sainsbury's magazine RECIPE

HEAT
SERVES 4
PREP TIME 10 mins
COOK TIME
30-35 mins

Caribbean hot vegetable curry

A spicy hot-pot of sweet potatoes, carrots, cabbage and chickpeas. Add a dash of hot pepper sauce if you like it really fiery

2 tbsp vegetable oil

1 onion, finely chopped

2 cloves garlic, crushed

1 tsp fresh thyme leaves

2 tsp hot curry powder by Sainsbury's

1 tsp ground coriander

1 tsp garam masala

1 Scotch bonnet chilli, deseeded and finely chopped

2 large sweet potatoes, peeled and cut into chunks

3 carrots, peeled and cut into chunks

500ml vegetable stock, made with 1 stock cube

½ white cabbage, trimmed and shredded

215g tin chickpeas by Sainsbury's, drained and rinsed

1 large red pepper, deseeded and cut into chunks

390g carton chopped tomatoes by Sainsbury's

40g creamed coconut, crumbled

100g bag young leaf spinach by Sainsbury's

1 tsp hot pepper sauce by Sainsbury's (optional)

1   Heat the oil in a large pan over a medium heat. Add the onion and garlic, and fry for 5 mins, until softened but not brown. Add all the herbs and spices and the chilli, and cook for 1-2 mins, stirring.

2   Add the sweet potatoes and carrots, then pour in the vegetable stock. Cover and simmer for 10-15 mins, then add the cabbage, chickpeas, pepper, tomatoes and creamed coconut. Simmer, uncovered, for a further 10 mins until all the vegetables are just tender and the sauce has thickened.

3   Stir in the spinach leaves and cook for a further 1-2 mins, until the leaves have wilted. Season to taste, then add the hot pepper sauce, if using.

Per serving: 1823kJ/435kcal (22%), 14.6g fat (21%), 7.2g saturates (36%), 26.3g sugars (29%), 1.26g salt (21%)

Devil's curry

A popular dish in Malaysia, devil's curry has tamarind and a splash of vinegar added for a tangy flavour. This veggie version is especially good

2 tbsp vegetable oil

2 tsp mustard seeds

1 large onion, roughly chopped

2 red chillies, very finely chopped

6 tbsp rendang paste (p10) or 190g jar rendang paste by Sainsbury's

1 tbsp tamarind paste

2 medium potatoes, peeled and cut into 2cm cubes

1 small butternut squash, peeled, deseeded and cut into 2cm cubes

2-3 red bird eye chillies by Sainsbury's, left whole and pierced with a tip of a knife (see cook's tip)

150g fine beans, trimmed

1 large red pepper, deseeded and cut into chunks

396g pack tofu, drained and cut into 2cm cubes

2 tbsp white wine vinegar

Small handful fresh coriander, chopped, plus extra leaves to garnish

1 Heat the oil in a large casserole over a medium-high heat. Add the mustard seeds and fry for 1-2 mins, until they start to pop. Add the onion and chillies, and fry for 5-6 mins, stirring frequently, until the onion is soft and golden.

2 Stir in the rendang and tamarind pastes, and cook for 1-2 mins. Add the potatoes and squash, and stir to coat in the pastes. Pour in enough cold water to barely cover and add the bird eye chillies. Season to taste. Bring to the boil, then reduce the heat, cover and simmer for 20 mins.

3 Add the beans and pepper to the casserole, and simmer, uncovered, for 10 mins, stirring occasionally, until the vegetables are just tender and the liquid has reduced a little. Add the tofu and simmer for 5 mins, then stir in the vinegar and coriander. Serve garnished with extra coriander leaves.

Per serving: 1521kJ/363kcal (18%), 14.1g fat (20%), 3.4g saturates (17%), 15.2g sugars (17%), 0.08g salt (1%)

Cook's tip
The bird eye chillies will impart an extra-hot flavour to this curry – unless you have a very high chilli heat tolerance, it's best not to eat the chillies themselves.

Split pea & vegetable sambar

This mildly spiced split pea and vegetable curried
stew goes really well with the onion parathas on p159

200g yellow split peas, rinsed and drained
1 onion, finely sliced
2 cloves garlic, crushed
2 tomatoes, roughly chopped
2 tbsp madras paste (p9) or 4 tbsp
madras paste by Sainsbury's
1 large potato, peeled and diced

1 small aubergine, trimmed and diced
100g frozen peas
2 tbsp vegetable oil
1 tsp cumin seeds
2 tsp mustard seeds
8 fresh curry leaves, washed
Fresh coriander leaves, to garnish

1   Put the split peas, onion, garlic, tomatoes and madras paste in a large saucepan
    with 1.2 litres water. Bring to the boil, skim off any impurities from the surface,
    then cover and simmer for 25 mins, until the split peas are tender.

2   Use a hand blender to purée the mixture until smooth. Stir in the potato and
    aubergine, then simmer for 15-20 mins, until the vegetables are tender, adding
    the frozen peas for the last 5 mins of cooking time. Season to taste.

3   Heat the oil in a frying pan over a medium heat and fry the cumin and mustard
    seeds for 1 min. Add the curry leaves and fry for 15-20 seconds, until aromatic.
    Stir the hot spicy oil into the lentil mixture and garnish with fresh coriander
    leaves. This is great served with onion parathas (p159), if you like.

**Per serving of curry without onion parathas: 1661kJ/395kcal (20%), 9g fat
(13%), 0.9g saturates (5%), 9g sugars (10%), 0.31g salt (5%)**

Cook's tip
You can vary the vegetables you use in this recipe – try
diced carrots and chopped green beans or okra instead
of the potatoes and peas.

HEAT

SERVES 4
PREP TIME 15-20
mins, plus 1-2 hours
marinating
COOK TIME
10-15 mins

Tandoori vegetable chapatti wraps

Try this brilliant idea for an easy dinner or lunch – spicy
chargrilled vegetables in a warm chapatti with a cooling mint raita

---

4 tbsp tandoori paste (p9), or 4 tbsp
shop-bought tandoori paste
150g low-fat natural yogurt
2 tbsp lemon juice
1 red and 1 yellow pepper, deseeded and
cut into strips
4 baby aubergines, trimmed and
quartered lengthways

4 baby courgettes, trimmed and
quartered lengthways
100g baby corn, halved lengthways
1 small red onion, thinly sliced
6cm piece cucumber, coarsely grated
Small handful fresh coriander, chopped
4 chapattis (p159)
½ quantity raita (p161)
Lemon wedges, to serve

---

1 Put the tandoori paste in a non-metallic bowl, add the yogurt and 1 tbsp lemon
   juice, then season to taste. Add the peppers, aubergines, courgettes and baby
   corn, and toss well to coat in the marinade. Cover and marinate in the fridge for
   1-2 hours.

2 Preheat the grill to medium-hot. Remove the vegetables from the marinade and
   spread out on a large grill pan. Cook under a medium-hot grill for 10-15 mins,
   turning frequently, until the vegetables are tender.

3 Meanwhile, in a bowl, mix together the red onion, cucumber, coriander and
   remaining lemon juice.

4 Warm the chapattis in a dry frying pan over a medium heat for 1 min on
   each side.

5 Divide the tandoori vegetables between the warmed chapattis. Top with the
   onion and cucumber mix, and drizzle over the raita. Serve with lemon wedges for
   squeezing. To eat, roll up the chapattis to enclose the vegetables and raita.

Per serving: 1555kJ/370kcal (19%), 12.3g fat (18%), 3.8g saturates (19%),
16.3g sugars (18%), 0.8g salt (13%)

Sides

Rice dishes

A curry isn't complete without rice! You can serve most of our recipes with plain steamed or boiled basmati rice, but try our variations, too. All these recipes serve 4. You'll also find a recipe for Thai sticky rice on p40

Jeera rice

This quick and simple fragrant side dish can be used as the base for a whole host of different rice accompaniments

PREP TIME: 5 mins, plus 5 mins standing time
COOK TIME: 15 mins

250g basmati rice
1 tbsp sunflower oil
2 tsp cumin seeds
Fresh coriander leaves, to garnish

---

1   Rinse the rice in a sieve until the water runs clear. Gently heat the oil in a medium saucepan, add the cumin seeds and cook for 1 min.

2   Add the rice and fry gently, stirring, for 1-2 mins, until all the grains are coated in oil. Add 500ml water and bring to the boil. Turn down the heat to a gentle simmer, cover and cook for 10 mins, until all the water is absorbed and dimples appear on the surface of the rice. Don't lift the pan lid or stir the rice.

3   Remove the pan from the heat and leave to stand for 5 mins. Fluff up the rice with a fork and garnish with the coriander leaves just before serving.

Per serving: 1035kJ/245kcal (12%), 3.3g fat (5%), 0.5g saturates (3%), <0.5g sugars (<1%), <0.01g salt (<1%)

Pilau rice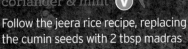

Follow the jeera rice recipe, replacing the cumin seeds with 1 bay leaf, 3 whole cloves, 2-3 cardamom pods and 1 cinnamon stick. To add a little colour (optional), just before leaving to stand add a couple of drops of red or pink and yellow food colouring (do not stir), then cover and leave to stand for 5 mins. Fluff up the rice grains with a fork before serving and remove the whole spices, if you like.

» Per serving: 1031kJ/244kcal (12%), 3.2g fat (5%), 0.5g saturates (3%), <0.5g sugars (<1%), <0.01g salt (<1%)

Spicy basmati rice with coriander & mint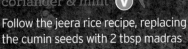

Follow the jeera rice recipe, replacing the cumin seeds with 2 tbsp madras paste (p9). Continue from step 2. Stir through a small handful of chopped coriander and mint before serving.

Per serving: 1071kJ/253kcal (13%), 4g fat (6%), 0.6g saturates (3%), <0.5g sugars (<1%), 0.01g salt (<1%)

Mushroom rice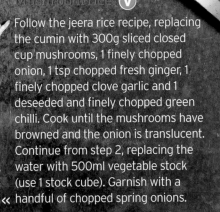

Follow the jeera rice recipe, replacing the cumin with 300g sliced closed cup mushrooms, 1 finely chopped onion, 1 tsp chopped fresh ginger, 1 finely chopped clove garlic and 1 deseeded and finely chopped green chilli. Cook until the mushrooms have browned and the onion is translucent. Continue from step 2, replacing the water with 500ml vegetable stock (use 1 stock cube). Garnish with a handful of chopped spring onions.

Per serving: 1202kJ/284kcal (14%), 4.2g fat (6%), 1g saturates (5%), 3.3g sugars (4%), 1.01g salt (17%)

Saffron rice

Soak a large pinch of saffron strands in 125ml water. Follow the jeera rice recipe, replacing the cumin seeds with 1 bay leaf, 3 whole cloves, 2-3 cardamom pods and 1 tsp fennel seeds. Continue from step 2, adding 375ml water and the saffron liquid instead of 500ml water. Fluff up with a fork and remove the whole spices before serving, if you like.

Per serving: 1035kJ/245kcal (12%), 3.3g fat (5%), 0.5g saturates (3%), <0.5g sugars (<1%), <0.01g salt (<1%)

Bread

Whether you're mopping up a luscious sauce with a naan, chapatti or roti, breads play an important role in the curry experience – and they're easier to make than you might think. Here are a few to try

Mini naan breads ⓥ

MAKES 4
PREP TIME: 15-20 mins, plus 30 mins resting time
COOK TIME: 4-6 mins

250g plain flour, plus extra for dusting
½ tsp baking powder
½ tsp salt
2 tsp caster sugar
1 tbsp vegetable oil, plus extra for brushing
110-150ml semi-skimmed milk

---

1   Tip the flour, baking powder, salt and sugar into a large bowl and mix well to combine. Stir in the vegetable oil, then, using your hands, gradually knead in the milk until the dough comes together and is only slightly sticky. Turn the dough out onto a work surface dusted with flour and knead until soft and stretchy (this will take up to 10 mins), adding more flour to the work surface if the dough is too sticky to work with. Return the dough to the bowl, cover with a damp cloth and set aside.

2   Preheat a baking sheet under a medium-hot grill for 4-5 mins. Divide the dough into 4 pieces (or 2 if you want to make large naan) and roll into balls. Flatten each ball with your hand, then roll out to a teardrop shape approximately 3mm thick.

3   Brush the tops with a little oil and place 2, oiled-side up, on the hot baking sheet. Grill for 1-2 mins, until dark patches appear. Turn the naans over, brush with a little more oil and grill for a further 1 min. Repeat with the remaining naans.

4   Wrap the cooked naans in foil for a few mins – the steam will make them soft and springy.

Per naan: 1230kJ/291kcal (15%), 5.1g fat (7%), 0.7g saturates (4%), 5.3g sugars (6%), 0.82g salt (14%)

Chapattis

MAKES 8
PREP TIME: 20 mins, plus 30 mins resting time
COOK TIME: 10 mins

300g chapatti flour by Sainsbury's, plus extra for dusting
1 tsp salt
3 tbsp vegetable oil

---

1 Sift the flour and salt into a mixing bowl, stir in the vegetable oil, then slowly add 200-240ml lukewarm water, stirring with one hand, until the dough starts to come together. Tip onto a lightly floured work surface and knead for 5 mins, until smooth.

2 Cover the dough with a damp tea towel and set aside to rest for 30 mins. Divide into 8 pieces, shape into balls and roll out to 15cm circles.

3 Cook each chapatti, one at a time, over a medium heat in a dry non-stick frying pan for about 1 min on each side, until browned in places. Alternatively, grill 2 chapattis at a time under a very hot grill for 30 seconds on each side. When they're cooked, wrap in foil and cook the remaining dough circles in the same way.

Per serving (2 chapattis): 1343kJ/ 320kcal (16%), 9.2g fat (13%), 0.7g saturates (4%), 1.6g sugars (2%), 1.23g salt (21%)

Variations:

Quick onion parathas V

1 Follow the chapatti recipe, substituting half the chapatti flour with plain flour. At the end of step 1, divide and shape the dough into 8 balls, then roll to 10cm circles on a floured surface. Spoon 1 tbsp chopped red onions onto the centre of each circle, dust with a little garam masala and flour and bring the edges together to join in the centre. Flatten, then roll to a 15cm circle on the floured surface.

2 Heat an oiled shallow heavy-based frying pan over a medium heat. Cook each paratha for 30 seconds, until light brown spots appear underneath, brush the top with a little extra vegetable oil, turn and cook for a further 30 seconds. Repeat for a further 15 seconds each side. Wrap the cooked parathas in a clean tea towel to keep them warm while cooking the rest.

Per serving (2 parathas): 1584kJ/ 377kcal (19%), 11.6g fat (17%), 0.9g saturates (5%), 3.5g sugars (4%), 1.23g salt (21%)

Roti V

1 Follow the chapatti recipe but at step 1 add only 150ml lukewarm water. Continue until the end of step 2. Brush each circle of dough with melted unsalted butter, then roll each one up like a rug. Take one end of each 'rug' and roll that up to make a tight coil of dough. Place, spiral facing up, on a floured work surface and flatten with the palm of your hand. Roll out to a 20cm circle. Repeat with the remaining dough balls.

2 Cook each roti over a medium heat in a large non-stick frying pan for about 1 min each side, until the surface bubbles and the base is browned in places. If the dough puffs up, press it down with a wooden spatula and keep it moving in the pan to stop it burning. Serve immediately, brushed with a little melted unsalted butter.

Per serving (2 rotis): 1575kJ/376kcal (19%), 15.4g fat (22%), 4.4g saturates (22%), 1.6g sugars (2%), 1.23g salt (21%)

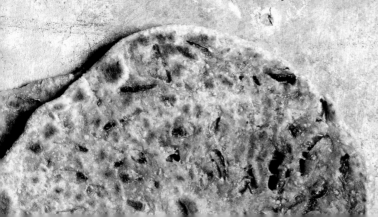

Pickles & relishes

Many of our curries will go down even better with a bowl of pickle, chutney, raita or relish on the side. Here's how to make them

Lime pickle

MAKES 2 x 350ml jars
PREP TIME: 20 mins, plus 2 days salting
COOK TIME: 30 mins

---

8 limes
2 tsp salt
1 tbsp vegetable oil
1 tbsp mustard seeds
4 cloves garlic, crushed
2cm piece fresh ginger, grated
2 tsp ground cumin
2 tsp ground fenugreek
1 tsp hot chilli powder
75g light brown soft sugar
3 tbsp white wine vinegar

You will also need:
2 x 350ml sterilised jars with lids (see cook's tip, opposite)

---

1   Cut each lime into 8 wedges, then halve each wedge. Place in a large clean lidded jar, sprinkle with the salt, then screw on the lid. Shake the jar to coat the limes in the salt. Put in a cool dry place for 2 days, shaking the jar every so often.

2   Heat the oil in a large saucepan over a medium heat and fry the mustard seeds for a few seconds until they start to pop. Add the garlic, ginger, cumin, fenugreek and chilli powder. Cook for about 1 min, stirring, until aromatic.

3   Stir in the salted limes, sugar, vinegar and 120ml water. Bring to the boil, reduce the heat and simmer for 25-30 mins, or until thickened, stirring occasionally.

4   Spoon into sterilised jars and seal while still hot. Store for a few days before using to allow the flavours to develop. Unopened, the pickle will keep in a cool, dry place for up to 3 months; once open, chill and use within 2 weeks.

Per tbsp: 102kJ/24kcal (1%), 0.8g fat (1%), <0.1g saturates (<1%), 3.8g sugars (4%), 0.49g salt (8%)

Mango chutney V

MAKES about 3½ x 500ml jars
(1.7kg in total)

PREP TIME: 35 mins
COOK TIME: 2 hours 15 mins

---

2 tbsp sunflower oil
1 tbsp panch phoron (Indian 5-spice – p187)
1 onion, thinly sliced
100g fresh ginger, peeled and grated
8 large ripe mangoes, peeled, stones removed and flesh cut into rough chunks
250ml white wine vinegar
500g golden caster sugar

You will also need:
4 x 500ml sterilised jars with lids (see cook's tip, right)

---

1 Heat the oil in a large pan over a medium heat, stir in the panch phoron and fry for 1-2 mins, until lightly toasted. Add the onion and fry for 5-6 mins, until softened. Stir in the ginger and cook, stirring, for a further 5 mins, until the onion is golden.

2 Add the mango and 500ml water to the onion and spices, cover and cook for 35-40 mins, until the mango is pulpy. Stir in the vinegar and sugar, then bubble, uncovered, for 30 mins, stirring frequently.

Reduce the heat and cook for 1 hour, or until thickened, stirring every so often.

Set aside to cool slightly, then spoon into sterilised jars. Seal while hot. Unopened, the chutney will keep in a cool, dry place for up to 3 months; once opened, chill and use within 2 weeks.

Per tbsp: 138kJ/33kcal (2%), <0.5g fat (<1%), <0.1g saturates (<1%), 6.8g sugars (8%), <0.01g salt (<1%)

Raita V

SERVES 4
PREP TIME 10 mins

½ cucumber, coarsely grated
400g Greek-style natural yogurt
Small handful mint leaves, shredded
½ tsp roasted cumin powder
1 tbsp lemon juice

---

1 In a sieve, use the back of a spoon to squeeze the excess water from the cucumber. Transfer to a bowl.

2 Add the remaining ingredients and mix. Season to taste. Serve or cover and chill for up to 2 days.

Per serving: 264kJ/64kcal (3%), 4.7g fat (7%), 3g saturates (15%),

2.9g sugars (3%), <0.08g salt (1%)

Kachumber V

SERVES 4
PREP TIME 15 mins

---

4 tomatoes, finely diced
½ cucumber, finely diced
½ red onion, finely chopped
1 green chilli, deseeded and finely chopped
Small handful fresh coriander, finely chopped
½ tsp cumin seeds, crushed
Juice of 1 lemon

Mix all the ingredients in a bowl, then season to taste. Cover and chill for up to 24 hours.

Per serving: 151kJ/36kcal (2%), <0.5g fat (<1%), <0.1g saturates (<1%), 4.9g sugars (5%), 0.02g salt (<1%)

To sterilise jars, wash jars and lids in warm, soapy water and rinse well. Dry with a clean tea towel, then place the jars in an oven preheated to 180°C, fan 160°C, gas 4 for 5 mins.

Indian side dishes

Make a feast of it with a vegetable side dish or two to serve alongside your curry – after all, variety is the spice of life

Saag paneer   V

HEAT
SERVES 4
PREP TIME: 10 mins
COOK TIME: 15 mins

2 tbsp vegetable oil
1 onion, thinly sliced
2 cloves garlic, crushed
1 tsp ground cumin
1 tsp ground coriander
½ tsp hot chilli powder
½ tsp ground turmeric
227g pack paneer cheese, cubed
260g young spinach

1 Heat the oil in a large deep frying pan and fry the onion over a medium-high heat for 5 mins, until softened. Add the garlic and spices, season and cook for a further 1-2 mins, then stir in 6 tbsp water.

2 Add the paneer and stir to coat in the onion and spice mixture. Cook for 5 mins, stirring occasionally. Add the spinach to the pan with another 4 tbsp water. Cook gently for a further 1-2 mins, stirring frequently, until the spinach has just wilted. Season to taste.

Per serving: 1198kJ/289kcal (15%), 21.6g fat (31%), 10.6g saturates (53%), 3g sugars (3%), 0.04g salt (1%)

Cabbage poriyal   V

HEAT
SERVES 4
PREP TIME: 10 mins
COOK TIME: 10-15 mins

2 tbsp vegetable oil
1 tsp mustard seeds
2cm piece fresh ginger, peeled and grated
1 green chilli, deseeded and finely chopped
½ tsp ground turmeric
3 fresh curry leaves, washed
1 small white cabbage, trimmed and finely shredded
¼ tsp salt
100g pack fresh coconut pieces by Sainsbury's, grated

1 Heat the oil in a large frying pan or wok and fry the mustards seeds for 1-2 mins until they start to pop. Add the ginger, chilli, turmeric and curry leaves and fry for 1 min.

2 Add the cabbage and toss to coat in the oil, then stir in the salt and 4 tbsp water. Cover and cook for 4-5 mins, until the cabbage is almost tender. Uncover and cook over a high heat for further 5 mins, until any liquid has evaporated, stirring occasionally. Stir in the grated coconut and season to taste.

Per serving: 791kJ/191kcal (10%), 13g fat (19%), 6.6g saturates (33%), 10.7g sugars (12%), 0.05g salt (1%)

Tarka dhal

HEAT
SERVES 4
PREP TIME: 10 mins
COOK TIME: about 1 hour

2 tbsp vegetable oil
1 onion, chopped
4cm piece fresh ginger,
peeled and grated
4 cloves garlic, 2 crushed
and 2 thinly sliced
1 tsp hot chilli powder
1 tsp ground turmeric
1 tsp cumin seeds
250g dried yellow split peas,
rinsed in cold water until the
water runs clear
2 large tomatoes, chopped
1 red chilli, quartered and deseeded

1 Heat half the oil in a large deep
pan, add the onion and fry over a
high heat for 5 mins. Stir in the
ginger and crushed garlic, and fry
gently until golden. Add the chilli
powder, turmeric and half the
cumin seeds. Fry for a further min.

2 Add the split peas and 900ml
water and bring to the boil. Add
the tomatoes and red chilli, cover
and simmer for 40 mins, stirring
occasionally. Season to taste, then
simmer, uncovered, for a further
10-15 mins, until the lentils are
tender and the liquid has reduced.

3 Heat the remaining oil in a small
pan and fry the sliced garlic and
remaining cumin seeds over a high
heat until the garlic is golden.
Ladle the dhal into warmed bowls
and pour over the spiced oil.

Per serving: 627kJ/150kcal (8%),
5.7g fat (8%), 0.4g saturates (2%),
5g sugars (6%), 0.03g salt (1%)

Bombay potatoes

SERVES 4
PREP TIME: 10 mins
COOK TIME: about 20 mins

500g new potatoes, halved (larger
ones quartered)
2 tbsp oil
¼ tsp mustard seeds
½ tsp cumin seeds
1 large onion, thinly sliced
1cm piece fresh ginger, peeled
and grated
½ tsp hot chilli powder
½ tsp garam masala
Small handful fresh coriander,
roughly chopped

---

1 Bring a large pan of water to the
   boil and add the potatoes. Cook for
   5-7 mins – they should still be quite
   firm. Drain well.

2 Meanwhile, heat the oil in a large
   deep frying pan over a medium
   heat. Add the mustard and cumin
   seeds, and fry until they start to
   pop. Add the onion and ginger and
   fry over a medium heat for 5-6
   mins, until the onions are soft and
   beginning to brown.

3 Stir in the parboiled potatoes,
   chilli powder and garam masala.
   Cook over a medium heat for
   5 mins, stirring occasionally.
   Stir in 4 tbsp water (add a little
   more if the potatoes are sticking),
   then cover and cook for a further 5
   mins, until the potatoes are golden
   and tender.

4 Remove the pan lid and cook over
   a high heat for a further 1-2 mins,
   until the potatoes are crisp around
   the edges. Season to taste.

**Per serving: 646kJ/154kcal (8%),
6g fat (9%), 0.5g saturates (3%),
3.5g sugars (4%), 0.05g salt (1%)**

Variation:
Aloo gobi

1 Follow the Bombay potatoes
   recipe, adding 400g cauliflower
   florets to the pan of boiling water
   with the potatoes for the last
   2 mins of the cooking time

2 Double the mustard and cumin
   seeds and continue with step 2.

**Per serving: 815kJ/194kcal (10%),
7.1g fat (10%), 0.7g saturates (4%),
6g sugars (7%), 0.08g salt (1%)**

Bhindi masala (1 of 5 a day) (V)

SERVES 4
PREP TIME: 10 mins
COOK TIME: about 20 mins

1 tbsp vegetable oil
1 large onion, chopped
2cm piece fresh ginger, peeled
and chopped
2 tsp mustard seeds
1 tsp cumin seeds
450g okra, trimmed and sliced into
1cm pieces
¼ tsp turmeric powder
1 tsp hot chilli powder
3 fresh curry leaves, washed

1. Heat the oil in a large deep lidded frying pan, add the onion and ginger, and cook for 5 mins, until the onion is translucent. Push the onions to one side and add the mustard and cumin seeds. Once they begin to pop, add the okra and stir-fry over a medium heat for 3-5 mins.

2. Add the turmeric and chilli powder and mix well to coat the okra in the spices. Reduce the heat to low, cover and cook, stirring occasionally, for 8-10 mins, until the okra is just tender (add a little more water if it starts to stick).

Per serving: 400kJ/96kcal (5%), 4.4g fat (6%), 0.6g saturates (3%), 5.2g sugars (6%), 0.05g salt (1%)

Spiced carrot & radish salad (1 of 5 a day) (V)

SERVES 4
PREP TIME: 15 mins, plus soaking and chilling time
COOK TIME: 1-2 mins

25g sultanas
2 tsp cumin seeds
1 tsp coriander seeds, lightly crushed
3 medium carrots, peeled and
coarsely grated
200g radishes, trimmed and thinly sliced
Juice and zest of 1 lemon
Handful fresh mint leaves, larger
leaves torn
1 tbsp olive oil

1. Put the sultanas in a small heatproof bowl and cover with boiling water. Leave to soak for 15 mins, then drain.

2. Heat a heavy-based frying pan until hot, then add the cumin and coriander seeds, and dry-fry over a medium heat for 1-2 mins, until lightly toasted.

3. Put the carrots and radishes in a bowl with the drained sultanas, toasted seeds, lemon juice and zest and mint. Toss well to mix, chill for 30 mins, then drizzle with the oil and toss again before serving.

Per serving: 352kJ/84kcal (4%), 3.2g fat (5%), 0.5g saturates (3%), 10.9g sugars (12%), 0.05g salt (1%)

Desserts

Fruit chaat

This colourful fruit salad contains just a hint of spice, and makes for
a wonderfully refreshing dessert after a spicy main course

1 apple, peeled, cored and sliced

2 bananas, peeled and sliced

Juice of 1 lemon

300g pineapple, peeled, cored and diced

1 mango, peeled, stone removed and
flesh diced

100g pack pomegranate seeds
by Sainsbury's

2 tsp light brown soft sugar

Zest of 1 orange

1 tsp cumin seeds

¼ tsp garam masala

Pinch of chilli powder

Fresh mint leaves, finely sliced, plus extra
leaves to decorate

1 In a large non-metallic bowl, mix the apple and bananas with the lemon juice,
then stir together with the other fruits, the sugar and the orange zest.

2 Toast the cumin seeds in a small pan over a low-medium heat for 2-3 mins, until
just turning golden. Remove from the heat immediately and grind to a fine
powder in a spice grinder (or use a pestle and mortar). Mix with the remaining
spices and gently fold through the fruit with the sliced mint.

3 Decorate with the remaining mint leaves to serve.

Per serving: 432kJ/102kcal (5%), 0.6g fat (1%), <0.1g saturates
(<1%), 19.7g sugars (22%), <0.01g salt (<1%)

Chai tea

Slowly bring 500ml water and 300ml full-fat milk to
the boil with 4 lightly crushed cardamom pods, a few
whole cloves, 1 cinnamon stick, 1 star anise and a few
black peppercorns. Simmer for 2-3 mins then add 3
Assam tea bags and remove from the heat. Cover
and infuse for 2-3 mins. Remove the tea bags, cover
and for leave for another 3 mins. Sweeten as desired..
SERVES 4 Prep time: 5 mins
Per serving: 208kJ/50kcal (3%), 2.8g fat (4%), 1.7g saturates
(9%), 3.5g sugars (4%), 0.11g salt (2%)

desserts

Caribbean rum cake

You'll find this cake all over the Caribbean, where it's a popular gift for tourists to bring home. Use good quality rum for authentic flavour

SERVES 12
PREP TIME
30 mins, plus
30 mins soaking
COOK TIME
40-45 mins

125g unsalted butter, plus extra for greasing
50g walnuts, finely chopped
200g caster sugar
4 medium eggs
275g self-raising flour, sifted
75ml semi-skimmed milk
100ml vegetable oil
1 tsp Taste the Difference Madagascan vanilla extract

3 tbsp dark rum
1 tbsp icing sugar, for dusting

FOR THE RUM SYRUP
50g unsalted butter
100g caster sugar
2 tbsp dark rum

1 Grease a 1.5-2 litre bundt tin (or use a 23cm round tin) and scatter 25g of the walnuts all over the sides of the tin. Preheat the oven to 180°C, fan 160°C, gas 4.

2 Put the 125g butter and sugar in a large bowl and beat together with an electric whisk until light and fluffy. Beat in the eggs, one by one, adding 1 tbsp of the flour with each egg. Fold in the remaining flour.

3 Add the milk, oil, vanilla extract and rum, then fold in gently. Pour the mixture into the tin and bake for 40-45 mins (35-40 mins if you're using a 23cm round tin), until risen and golden, and a skewer inserted into the cake comes out clean. Leave in the tin on a wire rack for 10 mins, then turn the cake out onto the wire rack and leave to cool completely.

4 Meanwhile, make the syrup. Put the butter, sugar, rum and 4 tbsp water in a pan and place over a low heat. Heat for 2-3 mins, until the butter has melted and the sugar has dissolved. Turn up the heat and bring to the boil. Simmer for 2-3 mins, until the syrup has reduced slightly, then remove from the heat.

5 Gently return the cold cake back to the clean cake tin and pierce all over with a skewer. Slowly spoon over the syrup, making sure most of it goes into the holes and not just down the sides of the cake. Leave to soak for 30 mins, then turn out and serve scattered with the remaining walnuts and a dusting of icing sugar.

Per serving: 1797kJ/431kcal (22%), 24.5g fat (35%), 8.6g saturates (43%), 26.5g sugars (29%), 0.25g salt (4%)

Carrot halva

This is a hugely popular dessert in India and Pakistan, especially at weddings and festivals. You can serve it warm or cold

20g unsalted butter

2 tbsp vegetable oil

10 carrots (about 1kg), peeled and grated

600ml whole milk

200g light brown soft sugar

50g ground almonds

Seeds from 6 cardamom pods, finely ground

30g raisins

Pinch of saffron strands, soaked in 1 tbsp warm milk for 5 mins

1 tbsp pistachio nuts, roughly chopped

1   Put the butter and oil in a large pan and heat gently until the butter has melted. Stir in the carrots and cook over a low heat for 15-20 mins, stirring occasionally. Stir in the milk and bring to the boil, then reduce the heat and simmer gently for 40 mins, until all the milk has been absorbed or evaporated. Stir occasionally to prevent the mixture sticking to the base of the pan.

2   Stir in the sugar, ground almonds and ground cardamom seeds, and continue to cook gently for a further 10 mins, stirring all the time. Once thickened, stir in the raisins and saffron milk. Serve warm, sprinkled with the chopped pistachios.

Per serving: 1683kJ/401kcal (20%), 15.8g fat (23%), 4.8g saturates (24%), 54g sugars (60%), 0.26g salt (4%)

Cook's tip
Toasting the pistachios brings another layer of flavour. Spread them out on a baking tray and roast at 180°C, fan 160°C, gas 4 for 5-10 mins, until lightly browned

MAKES 16
PREP TIME
20-25 mins, plus
3 hours soaking
COOK TIME
15-20 mins

Gulab jamun

Save these celebratory mini doughnut balls for an extra-special occasion

200g self-raising flour
Pinch of salt
35g caster sugar
25g unsalted butter, melted
75ml semi-skimmed milk, warmed
½ tbsp natural yogurt
Vegetable oil, for deep frying
½ tbsp pistachio nuts, finely chopped

FOR THE SYRUP
300g caster sugar
Pinch of saffron strands, soaked in 1 tbsp
hot water for 5 mins
Seeds of 10 cardamom pods, finely ground
1 tsp rose water

1   Put the flour, salt and sugar in a mixing bowl. Pour in the butter, milk and yogurt, and mix to form a soft dough. Roll into 16 walnut-sized balls. Make sure the balls are smooth and without cracks - this will ensure that they don't break up. It helps to gently wet your hands to do this.

2   Half fill a deep pan with the oil and heat to 180°C, or until a small piece of dough dropped into the hot oil rises to the surface and begins to brown in 30 seconds. Fry the balls, four at a time, for 3-4 mins, turning occasionally with a metal slotted spoon, until evenly browned all over. Remove with a slotted spoon and drain on kitchen paper.

3   Meanwhile, make the syrup. Put the sugar in a pan with 450ml water. Heat gently, stirring all the time, until the sugar has dissolved. Bring to the boil and bubble for 10-15 mins, until syrupy. Stir in the saffron water, cardamom and rosewater, then transfer to a heatproof bowl.

4   Put the fried balls in the syrup, cover and leave in a cool place to soak for up to 3 hours (see cook's tip). Serve cold, sprinkled with the pistachio nuts. To serve warm, transfer to a pan and reheat gently.

Per ball: 828kJ/197kcal (10%), 7.6g fat (11%), 1.3g saturates (7%), 21.3g sugars (24%), 0.12g salt (2%)

Cook's tip
The fried balls can be left in the syrup for longer than 3 hours, but put the bowl in the fridge after that time.

MAKES 8
PREP TIME 10 mins,
plus cooling and
4 hours freezing
COOK TIME
15 mins

Kulfi with pistachios & cashews

A traditional style of ice cream from India, kulfi is usually made from sweetened condensed milk. Enjoy as an occasional treat

410g tin evaporated milk by Sainsbury's
397g tin condensed milk
150ml single cream
Pinch of saffron strands

Seeds from 6 cardamom pods
75g cashew nuts (unsalted)
Vegetable oil, for greasing
25g pistachio nuts, roughly chopped

1 Put the evaporated and condensed milks, cream, cardamom and saffron in a large pan and bring to a very gentle simmer. Cook over a low heat for 10 mins, then remove from the heat and cool. Strain through a sieve into a clean bowl.

2 Meanwhile, put the cashews in a small pan and toast over a low heat for 2-3 mins, until just turning golden. Cool for 5 mins, then tip into a mini food processor and process for a few seconds to make fine crumbs. Stir into the milk mixture.

3 Half-fill 8 lightly greased lolly moulds (about 125ml capacity) with the mixture and freeze for 2 hours. Gently push a wooden lolly stick into the centre of each kulfi, then top up the moulds with the remaining mixture. Freeze for a further 2 hours, until fully set.

4 To remove the kulfi, dip the moulds very briefly into a bowl of hot water and turn out onto serving plates. Scatter over the pistachio nuts to serve.

Per kulfi: 1499kJ/358kcal (18%), 18.1g fat (26%), 8.2g saturates (41%), 35g sugars (39%), 0.41g salt (7%)

Cook's tips
If you want to make lollies but don't have lolly moulds, you can use darioles, ramekins or used (and cleaned) yogurt pots instead.

176

SERVES 4
PREP TIME 30 mins
COOK TIME 30 mins, plus at least 4-5 hours chilling

Tropical pannacotta with coconut snaps

This simple, elegant dessert looks so pretty and tastes divine. It's the perfect finale to any Indian- or Asian-inspired curry feast!

200ml single cream
275ml reduced fat coconut milk
140g caster sugar
3 leaves fine-leaf gelatine
100g natural yogurt
4 limes
1 ripe mango, peeled, stone removed and flesh thinly sliced

FOR THE COCONUT SNAPS
1 large egg, separated, white only
100g desiccated coconut
1 tsp sesame seeds
50g caster sugar
Oil, for greasing

1 Put the cream, coconut milk and 65g of the sugar in a pan, and bring to a simmer, stirring. Meanwhile, soak the gelatine leaves in a bowl of cold water.

2 Take the cream mixture off the heat. Squeeze the liquid out of the gelatine and add to the cream, stirring to dissolve. Cool, then stir in the yogurt. Pour into 4 x 175ml mini pudding basins. Cool, cover and chill for 4-5 hours or overnight.

3 Preheat the oven to 160°C, fan 140°C, gas 3. For the snaps, beat the egg white in a bowl until frothy, stir in the coconut, sesame seeds and sugar. Put tablespoons of the mixture onto an oiled baking tray lined with baking paper, lightly pressing them out - you should have about 16 biscuits. Bake for 15 mins, then press again to flatten and bake for 5 more mins. Transfer to a wire rack to cool.

4 Zest 2 of the limes and set aside. Juice all of the limes and, in a pan, dissolve the juice with the remaining sugar over a low heat. Increase the heat and bubble until syrupy, then set aside to cool.

5 Turn the pannacottas out onto plates (dip the pudding basins in a bowl of just-boiled water for 30 seconds to release, if necessary). Drizzle with the lime syrup and sprinkle with lime zest. Serve with the mango slices and coconut snaps.

Per serving: 1866kJ/446kcal (22%), 23.7g fat (34%), 17.3g saturates (87%), 49.9g sugars (55%), 0.15g salt (3%)

Sainsbury's
magazine
RECIPE

SERVES 4
PREP TIME 5-10
mins, plus at least
6 hours draining and
1-2 hours chilling

Shrikhand

Also known as the ambrosia of the gods, this yogurt-based dessert
is a luxuriously delicious way to end an Indian meal

2 x 500g pots low fat natural yogurt
by Sainsbury's

4 tbsp icing sugar

40g pistachio nuts, finely chopped

Seeds from 5 cardamom pods,
coarsely ground

Large pinch of saffron strands, soaked
in 2 tbsp hot semi-skimmed milk for 10 mins

1 Line a metal colander with a 30cm square of muslin cloth. Put the colander over
   a large bowl, making sure there is room for the liquid to drip out of the bottom of
   the colander. Pour the yogurt into the muslin, and tie the four corners together
   to enclose the yogurt. Leave to drain for 6 hours (or overnight) in the fridge.
   Remove from the fridge and discard the liquid that has drained into the bowl.

2 Tip the thickened yogurt into a clean bowl and whisk in the icing sugar until
   smooth. Fold in the two-thirds of the pistachio nuts, the cardamom seeds and
   nearly all the saffron milk. Cover and chill in the fridge for 1-2 hrs.

3 To serve, spoon into serving bowls and swirl through the rest of the saffron milk,
   then top with the remaining pistachio nuts.

Per serving: 768kJ/183kcal (9%), 5.9g fat (8%), 2g saturates (10%),
20.6g sugars (23%), <0.01g salt (<1%)

Cook's tip

You'll find muslin cloth (sometimes called butter
muslin) in good kitchenware shops, or look online.
For a speedier dessert, you can use a 500g pot of thick
Greek-style yogurt and skip method 1. The consistency
will be a little looser, but the taste will be just as good!

Thai coconut sorbet

Creamy coconut and zingy lime give this easy-to-make dessert its deliciously fresh flavour – with help from another unusual ingredient

100g caster sugar

2 fresh kaffir lime leaves, washed

400ml tin reduced fat coconut milk

25g desiccated coconut

4 basil leaves, thinly sliced

Juice and pared zest of 1 lime

1 Mix the sugar with 150ml water in a small saucepan and put over a low heat. Simmer gently, stirring, for 3-4 mins, until the sugar has dissolved, then increase the heat and boil for 2-3 mins. Add the lime leaves and set aside to cool.

2 Remove the lime leaves from the sugar syrup and add the coconut milk, desiccated coconut, basil and lime juice and stir to fully combine. Pour into a 1 litre freezable container and freeze for 4 hours. Break up the sorbet with a fork and freeze for a further 4 hours until firm. Serve in scoops or crushed in glasses with lime zest to garnish.

Per serving: 894kJ/214kcal (11%), 11g fat (16%), 9.5g saturates (48%), 26.3g sugars (29%), <0.01g salt (<1%)

Cook's tip
For a refreshing minty twist, use fresh mint leaves instead of basil.

Ingredients glossary

All of our recipes contain ingredients that are readily available at Sainsbury's. Find out more about what makes these products so special for curries

Cardam...

Asafoetida

Caraway seeds

Chilli powde...

Herb and spices: Indian subcontinent

Asafoetida
This is a fine yellowish powder ground from the dried resinous gum collected from three species of giant fennel plant. Its strong smell mellows when fried in oil, and when fully cooked it takes on a truffle-like flavour and a delicious roasted garlic aroma.

Black pepper/peppercorns
A tabletop favourite in Western cuisine, pepper or peppercorns add a spicy hit to dishes, as well as enhancing the taste of other ingredients. Pepper was in fact the main source of heat in all Indian dishes before the introduction of South American chillies in the 15th century, courtesy of the Portuguese. Black peppercorns are berries that are picked and dried when mature. Green and white peppercorns result from different harvesting times.

Caraway seeds
With their distinctive bitter, nutty flavour with sweet undertones, caraway seeds are in fact the dried fruits of a flowering herb. The caraway plant is a member of the carrot family, so a few seeds in a carrot or root-vegetable dish make a harmonious and welcome addition.

Cardamom
Each fragrant oval cardamom pod is filled with around 12 tiny dark brown or black seeds. Depending on their country of origin, cardamom seeds are likely to be stronger in either eucalyptus or floral-citrus flavours. Whichever dominates, the fresh notes are great for cutting through fattiness - thus, teaming cardamom with a creamy curry will let its flavour shine.

Chilli powder
This comes in hot, medium and mild, and is made by grinding dried chilli peppers to a powder. Add a teaspoon to plainer dishes to give another layer of flavour.

Cinnamon
Cinnamon is a very aromatic spice with a warm, sweet, citrus flavour. It's versatile, too, and can be used in both sweet and savoury dishes. The bark of the cassia tree is removed, dried and rolled up to make small tubes, which are sold as cinnamon sticks. Ground cinnamon is an integral part of garam masala.

Cloves
Dried cloves (the unopened red flower buds of the clove tree) can be used whole or ground. They have an extremely strong and aromatic flavour, with a fruity and sometimes sharp, bitter flavour. They are often paired with other spices to create a rounded flavour.

Coriander leaves
Their bittersweet taste is quite different to coriander seeds and they make an ideal flavour enhancer. They wilt and lose a little flavour if cooked, so it's best to add towards the end of cooking or use the leaves as a garnish.

Coriander seeds
Coriander seeds have a delicious citrus and slightly balsamic character, bringing a fragrant, subtle touch to curry powder blends and pastes. Once ground, the

Cloves

Fennel seeds

Cumin

Nigella seeds

Fenugreek

Mustard seeds

delicate peppery flavour of the seeds can fade quickly, so try filling a pepper mill with roasted coriander seeds and grinding them as needed.

Cumin
Cumin has a strong and distinctive flavour that is transformed by cooking. When the seeds are roasted and crushed, they release deliciously nutty, lemony notes and when fried in oil, they add a lively bite to your dishes.

Curry leaves
Often found in Southern Indian and Sri Lankan dishes, these dark green leaves are from a tree of the citrus family and release a wonderful nutty, lemony aroma when fried in hot oil.

Fennel seeds
This dried seed from the fennel herb has a strong aniseed flavour. They're often used in spiced sauces and pair well with lamb and vegetable dishes. In India they're fried or toasted, then eaten after a meal, as they are thought to aid digestion.

Fenugreek
Popular in Indian cookery, fenugreek seed has a tangy, slightly bitter taste and is often used in curries, pickles and sauces. The seeds are quite difficult to grind, so if a recipe calls for ground fenugreek, it's best to buy it ready prepared.

Mint
The coolest herb of them all, mint can be stirred into chopped cucumber and yogurt to calm even the fieriest of curries. This mint and yogurt accompaniment, called raita (see our recipe p161) in South Asia, boasts subtle variations in cuisines as varied as Greek and Indian.

Mustard seeds
White, yellow, brown or black, mustard seeds come from three different plants, with the sharp, biting flavour of black being the strongest and the white mustard seeds tending to be milder. Black or brown seeds are the mustard seeds of choice for Indian cooking. Fry gently to release their nutty, rather than fiery flavour.

Nigella seeds
The nigella plant is a member of the buttercup family. The mild peppery seeds are found in the head of the flowers. Try sprinkling over mini naan breads (p158) when grilling, but only add them after you have turned the breads once or they will fall off.

Nutmeg and mace
Native to Indonesian islands, nutmeg and mace come from the same tree – nutmeg being the nut and mace the aril, or outer casing. Add freshly grated nutmeg to aubergine dishes for a match made in heaven. Mace, with its milder flavour, is perfect for adding subtle nutmeg notes to fish dishes.

Paprika
This is made from a variety of sweet, mild pepper, which is ground to a red powder. The aroma of paprika tends to be subtle and smoky with slight caramel notes. Its deep red colour makes it an attractive garnish, while it also brings a distinct flavour to any dish it is added to.

185

Garam masala

Saffron

Tamarind paste

Turmeric

Saffron
Often called 'the spice of the gods', saffron has a rich, musky, honey aroma and adds a brilliant golden yellow colour. The dried stigmas of the saffron crocus, saffron requires a large cultivation area and hundreds of flowers to obtain even the smallest amount, hence it is the world's most expensive spice.

Tamarind
Sometimes known as the Indian date, tamarind is used as a spice and souring agent. The fruit is a long pod that contains a sour pulp full of seeds; the pulp can be processed to make a paste. Lending a sweet and sour note to Asian cuisine, tamarind extract is also a key ingredient in Worcestershire sauce.

Turmeric
Turmeric has been used in a wide range of Indian home remedies for many years. It's also an ingredient in classic Indian dishes such as kedgeree and dhal. With its distinctive yellow colour, it is often used instead of saffron, although it has quite a different peppery, musky flavour.

Herbs and spices:
Far East and South-East Asia

Kaffir lime leaves
The delicate citrus flavour of kaffir lime leaves make them ideal for fish and chicken dishes. You can buy both fresh and freeze-dried leaves in Sainsbury's. Freeze-dried leaves will keep in a sealed container for up to one year.

Lemon grass
A key ingredient in Far-Eastern cuisine, these woody stalks have a sweet, citrussy flavour that intensifies when cut or bashed, although lemon grass is also now easy to find as a convenient paste instore. Try experimenting by adding a touch to your favourite dishes for a Far-Eastern fusion flavour.

Sesame seeds
In Western and Indian cuisine we often find sesame seeds add a rounded toasty dimension to breads and pastries. They are also great lightly toasted and sprinkled over East Asian dishes (see our sticky rice recipe on p40).

Star anise
Shaped like an eight-pointed star and containing seeds with an aromatic aniseed flavour, star anise is widely used in Far Eastern cooking, where it's added to slow-cooked stews, curries and sauces to lend a warm, rounded flavour. Star anise is also added to flavour the stock used in Vietnamese pho and soup dishes. Pop a few whole star anise, a cinnamon stick and a couple of cardamom pods in your rice water when cooking and you'll add a deliciously aromatic layer.

Thai basil
An aniseed-flavoured herb perfect for Thai curries, Thai basil works particularly well combined with the citrus base of lemon grass. Available as a handy paste instore, it's ideal for keeping in the fridge to add a touch of authenticity to red curries or any other Thai dishes.

Herbs and spices:
Caribbean

Allspice
This spice is a good all-rounder. The dried berry of the West Indian allspice tree

Kaffir limes leaves

Ginger

Galangal pulp

Star anise

earns its name from its flavour, which is like a combination of cinnamon, nutmeg, cloves and pepper. Used in both sweet and savoury dishes, it adds a sweet, aromatic note to spicy Jamaican dishes such as jerk chicken, as well as pairing beautifully with richer meats such as game and lamb curry dishes.

Spice mixes

Chinese five spice
This combination of sweet, sour, bitter, pungent and salty spices are commonly used in Chinese and Vietnamese cooking. The spice mixture varies, but commonly includes cinnamon, peppercorns, star anise, cloves and fennel seeds.

Curry powder
A standard mix will include coriander seed, cumin, garlic, chilli powder, cardamom and black pepper, with varying degrees of chilli heat making a mild, medium or hot blend.

Garam masala
This mixture of ground spices, which is used as the base of a huge number of Indian dishes, can be made from scratch or bought ready-made. The amount of each spice used can vary from region to region and can be adapted to personal preference, although a standard mix is likely to include any combination of ground coriander seed, dill seed, cumin, turmeric, cinnamon, black pepper, cloves, ginger and cardamom.

Panch phoron
Literally meaning five spices, this mixture consists of the following seeds: cumin, black mustard (use yellow if black are unavailable), fenugreek (use powder if seeds are unavailable), nigella and fennel. Delicious in Indian potato dishes, it's also easy to assemble – simply measure out and combine the five different spice seeds and keep in an airtight jar.

Fruits, roots and bulbs

Chillies
There are more than 200 known varieties of chilli, the fruit of which vary greatly in size, colour and heat, although in general the smaller the chilli, the more potent its heat, while green and yellow chillies tend to be hotter than red ones. If you like hotter curries, leaves the seeds in.

Galangal
This root from the ginger family is widely used in South-East Asian cuisine, particularly Thai, Malaysian and Indonesian curries. Buy it fresh or in a jar as a paste; fresh galangal can be kept wrapped in cling film or in a paper bag for 2-3 weeks in the fridge.

Garlic
Adding garlic to meat, fish or vegetables draws and outlines their flavour, giving fellow ingredients definition. For a mild garlic flavour, infuse warm cooking oil with a whole clove. For something stronger, crush a peeled clove to a paste.

Ginger
Popular the world over, ginger is available fresh, dried, ground, glacé, pickled and preserved in syrup. Fresh ginger is predominantly used in our curry recipes and it has a lemony, woody and earthy quality, while dried ground ginger can pack a fiery punch.

Mirin

Sesame oil

Fish sauce

Gram flour

Oils and sauces

Fish sauce
This powerful thin brown liquid is indispensable in Thai kitchens, where it's known as nam pla. It's made by fermenting small whole fish, such as anchovies, in brine, although the fishy taste mellows to a delicate savoury flavour when cooked. You can also use it as a condiment to season Thai dishes.

Ghee
A clarified butter that originates in India, ghee is simmered until all the moisture evaporates and the milk solids begin to brown, giving the butter a nutty, caramel flavour and aroma. Because of its high saturated fat content, our recipes use vegetable oil instead of ghee but you can use it, if you prefer.

Groundnut oil
This useful oil is made from peanuts. It's virtually flavourless, retaining only a slightly nutty taste, which means it's ideal for enriching dishes without adding strong flavours. Another advantage of groundnut oil is that it has a high heat resistance, making it good for frying.

Mirin
A staple condiment in Japanese cooking, mirin is a sweetened rice wine with a slightly syrupy texture.

Rice vinegar
An essential in oriental cooking, rice vinegar is made from fermented rice. Chinese and especially Japanese vinegars are very mild and sweet.

Sesame oil
A flavoursome oil with a distinctive nutty, toasted taste. It's not recommended for frying, but drizzle it over oriental dishes or salads before serving.

Soy sauce
Made from fermented soya beans, salt, water and barley or wheat flour, soy sauce is an essential part of Japanese and Chinese cooking. Available in dark and light varieties, light is ideal for adding to soups, dips and vegetable dishes, whereas the dark version works well with stronger-flavoured dishes, such as beef and duck.

Storecupboard

Bamboo shoots
The tender shoots from the bamboo plant have a mild flavour and distinctive crunch, giving an authentic touch to curry dishes from South and South-East Asia and the Far East. Bamboo shoots are available tinned in Sainsbury's.

Bread flours
Flours such as chapatti (wholemeal wheat flour) and plain are commonly used for making Indian-style breads such as roti, chapatti and paratha (see p158). Other bread flours you can buy are gram (made from chickpeas) and rice flour (made from milled brown and white rice).

Chopped tomatoes
The ultimate versatile storecupboard staple, chopped tomatoes pop up in lamb

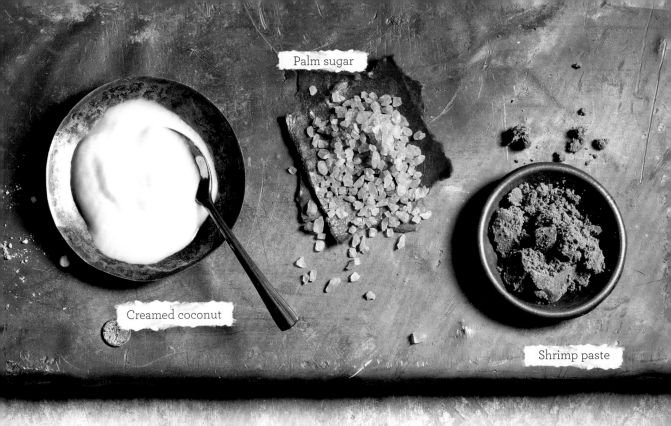

Palm sugar

Creamed coconut

Shrimp paste

rogan josh (p94), beef madras (p84), chicken vindaloo (p58) and a host of other tomato-based curries.

Coconut milk
An essential ingredient in both Caribbean and South-East Asian recipes, coconut milk adds a rich, creamy flavour and luscious texture to curry dishes. It has a high saturated fat content, but you can buy reduced-fat versions (the reduced-fat versions have a lower percentage coconut extract content). Give tins a good shake before opening them to mix the contents thoroughly.

Creamed coconut
Concentrated coconut that's been formed into a block. Grate or chop it, then let it melt into oriental and Caribbean dishes for a luxurious creamy flavour.

Desiccated coconut
Dried and shredded coconut is used as a garnish or ingredient in main course dishes, as well as a decoration and key

component of many Thai and Indian-style desserts and sweets.

Lentils
These fibre and protein-packed legumes are a key ingredient in Indian dhals and other vegetarian dishes. There are plenty of varieties, such as puy lentils, red, green and brown lentils. Some need to be soaked before using and others just need rinsing, then a longer cooking time. Or choose tinned, which are ready to use.

Noodles
Rice, wheat (udon) or egg noodles are used in some oriental curry dishes as a carbohydrate base for the curry sauce.

Palm sugar
Extracted from palm trees, this sugary syrup is made into granules, which you can buy instore and use to balance the flavours in curries and other dishes.

Rice
Rice is the staple accompaniment to the

majority of Indian, South-East Asian and oriental curries. There's a huge amount of different varieties available throughout the world, including jasmine, wild and long grain, but the main ones you'll need for these recipes are basmati and Thai sticky rice. Basmati is mainly used to accompany Indian dishes, while short grain rices, such as sticky rice and sushi rice, tend to be used more in Thai and oriental dishes. Turn to p156 for some interesting rice dishes to cook alongside your curries.

Shrimp paste
A common ingredient in South-East Asian dishes, shrimp paste is made from ground up shrimp with salt. It gives off a pungent smell, but added to cooking it lends depth and an exotic, authentic flavour.

Split peas
A good source of protein and fibre, dried peas are a staple of Indian dhal and other vegetarian dishes. Dried split peas usually need to be soaked before use.

Index

Index

All recipes have been tried, tested and tasted by Sainsbury's, so you can be sure of great results every time

Conversion table

Weights		Volume		Measurements		Oven temperatures		fan	gas
15g	½ oz	25ml	1 fl oz	2mm	¹⁄₁₆ in	110°C	90°C		
25g	1 oz	50ml	2 fl oz	3mm	⅛ in	120°C	100°C		½
40g	1½ oz	75ml	3 fl oz	4mm	⅙ in	140°C	120°C		1
50g	2 oz	100ml	4 fl oz	5mm	¼ in	150°C	130°C		2
60g	2½ oz	150ml	5 fl oz (¼ pint)	1cm	½ in	160°C	140°C		3
75g	3 oz	175ml	6 fl oz	2cm	¾ in	180°C	160°C		4
100g	3½ oz	200ml	7 fl oz	2.5cm	1 in	190°C	170°C		5
125g	4 oz	225ml	8 fl oz	3cm	1¼ in	200°C	180°C		6
150g	5 oz	250ml	9 fl oz	4cm	1½ in	220°C	200°C		7
175g	6 oz	300ml	10 fl oz (½ pint)	4.5cm	1¾ in	230°C	210°C		8
200g	7 oz	350ml	13 fl oz	5cm	2 in	240°C	220°C		9
225g	8 oz	400ml	14 fl oz	6cm	2½ in				
250g	9 oz	450ml	16 fl oz (¾ pint)	7.5cm	3 in				
275g	10 oz	600ml	20 fl oz (1 pint)	9cm	3½ in				
300g	11 oz	750ml	25 fl oz (1¼ pints)	10cm	4 in				
350g	12 oz	900ml	30 fl oz (1½ pints)	13cm	5 in				
375g	13 oz	1 litre	34 fl oz (1¾ pints)	13.5cm	5¼ in				
400g	14 oz	1.2 litres	40 fl oz (2 pints)	15cm	6 in				
425g	15 oz	1.5 litres	52 fl oz (2½ pints)	16cm	6½ in				
450g	1 lb	1.8 litres	60 fl oz (3 pints)	18cm	7 in				
500g	1 lb 2 oz			19cm	7½ in				
650g	1 lb 7 oz			20cm	8 in				
675g	1½ lb			23cm	9 in				
700g	1 lb 9 oz			24cm	9½ in				
750g	1 lb 11 oz			25.5cm	10 in				
900g	2 lb			28cm	11 in				
1kg	2 lb 4 oz			30cm	12 in				
1.5kg	3 lb 6 oz			32.5cm	13 in				
				35cm	14 in				

Sainsbury's food safety advice

General kitchen safety guidelines

- Wash your hands thoroughly before food preparation. If handling raw meat, fish or poultry, it's equally important to wash your hands after preparation, too.
- Keep raw food separate from ready-to-eat foods when you're preparing meals; use separate chopping boards and utensils or wash thoroughly between use.
- Washing raw chicken spreads bacteria around the kitchen via tiny splashes, which increases the risk of cross-contamination to other foods. The best way to destroy harmful bacteria is by cooking thoroughly, until piping hot throughout with no pink colour remaining in the flesh.
- Refer to ingredient packaging for full preparation and cooking instructions.

- Public health advice is to avoid consumption of raw or lightly looked eggs, especially for those vulnerable to infections, including pregnant women, babies and the elderly.
- Wash fresh vegetables, fruit and herbs (including any used for garnishing dishes) before use.
- When reheating leftovers, make sure they are piping hot throughout.

Freezing and defrosting

- Products can be frozen up to the use-by date (check labels to see if suitable to freeze).
- Defrost food overnight in the fridge (covered in a dish to avoid contaminating other products).

Refrigerating food

- Keep your fridge temperature below 5°C.
- To avoid cross-contamination, cover raw meat and poultry and store at the bottom of the fridge, separate from ready-to-eat food.
- When preparing food, keep out of the fridge for the shortest time possible.
- Cool down leftovers as quickly as possible then, once cooled, cover and put in the fridge and eat within two days.
- Clean your fridge regularly to ensure it remains hygienic and in good working condition.
- For tinned food, decant the contents into a non-metallic container and seal.

'Best before' and 'use-by' dates

- Food with a 'use-by' date goes off quite quickly and could pose a health risk if consumed after this date.
- Food with a 'best before' date is longer-lasting. It is safe to eat after this date but will not be at its best quality.

Recipe nutrition

The nutrition information on each recipe shown in this book has been calculated using Sainsbury's own-brand products and is based on 1 adult portion, assuming equal division of the recipe into the suggested number of servings.

Nutrition is calculated using each recipe's ingredients list only and does not include any sides, accompaniments or other serving suggestions mentioned in the method. The nutrition content will vary if other products are used or if the servings are not identical. Also, variations in cooking methods may affect the nutrition content.

The nutritional information on each recipe also includes the percentage of Reference Intakes (RIs) provided by a serving. RIs are a guide to the maximum amounts of calories, fat, saturates, sugars and salt an adult should consume in a day (based on an average female adult) and are as follows:

Energy or nutrient	Reference Intake per day
Energy	8400kJ/2000kcal
Total fat	70g
Saturates	20g
Total sugars	90g
Salt	6g

Seasoning: we're committed to promoting healthier eating and lowering salt in daily diets. As such we have worked hard to produce recipes that do not need as much (if any) salt seasoning. Note: recipe nutrition does not include any salt you add yourself.

For more information on food safety and nutrition, visit sainsburys.co.uk/livewellforless and sainsburys.co.uk/kitchensafety

Credits

Food
Food editor Angela Romeo
Assistant food editor Lottie Covell
Food assistant Nadine Brown

Recipes & food styling Angela Drake, Georgina Fuggle, Nichola Palmer, Mima Sinclair, Hannah Yeadon

Editorial
Head of content Helen Renshaw
Group Managing Editor Christine Faughlin
Editor Julie Stevens
Sub editor Ward Hellewell

Design & photography
Art director Dan Perry
Prop stylist Morag Farquhar
Photography Jonathan Kennedy
Sainsbury's Magazine photography Jonathan Gregson, Dan Jones, Martin Poole, Brett Stevens
Sainsbury's magazine recipes Emma Franklin, Lucy Jessop, Kat Mead, Sarah Randell
Additional photography David Munns
Additional stylists Sal Henley

Account management
Account manager Jo Brennan
Client director Andy Roughton

For Sainsbury's
Book team Phil Carroll, Lynne de Lacy, Robyn Haque, Tony Jagpal, Mavis Sarfo,
Nutrition Alastair McArthur
Product safety manager Nikki Mosley

Production
Production director Sophie Dillon
Colour origination F1 Colour Ltd

Special thanks to...
Shermin Ali, Jon Ashford, Patricia Baker, Francesca Clarke, Frances Ewings, Marcus Ludewig, Pam Price

seven.co.uk

Sainsbury's magazine

* Delicious triple-tested recipes your family will love

* Interesting and inspiring features

* Great fashion and beauty ideas

* Tempting offers and exciting competitions

LOVE ALL THIS AND WANT MORE?

If you subscribe to *Sainsbury's magazine* you'll get it delivered straight to your door before it hits the shops and benefit from exclusive gifts and offers, too! Visit **sainsburysmagazine.co.uk** for our latest great-value subscription offer

FSC MIX Paper from responsible sources FSC® C005461

© Produced by Seven Publishing on behalf of Sainsbury's Supermarkets Ltd, 33 Holborn, London EC1N 2HT. Published September 2014. All rights reserved. No part of this publication may be reproduced, stored in a retrieval system or transmitted in any form by any means - electronically, mechanically, via photocopying, recording or otherwise - without the prior written permission of Seven Publishing. Printed in Italy by Rotolito Lombarda. ISBN-13: 978-0-9928273-2-8